STRONGER
THAN SUGAR

7 Simple Steps to

Defeat Sugar Addiction,

Lift Your Mood and

Transform Your Health

By Joan Kent, Ph.D.

D1399908

TABLE OF CONTENTS

Introduction...7

So Who Am I, and Why Should You Listen To Me?................................ 9

Book 1:   The Basics of Sugar Addiction

Chapter 1:   Why Sugar Addiction Matters..15

Chapter 2:   Why Sugar Addiction Affects Some of Us More Than Others.....19

Chapter 3:   Sweet Tooth or Sugar Addiction: What's the Difference?...............23

Book 2:   Sugar and Your Brain

Chapter 4:   Why You Shouldn't Eat What You Crave...31

Chapter 5:   What Causes Sugar Cravings? (It's Not What You Think!)...........35

Chapter 6 :   Are You Eating These Protein Imposters? 61

Chapter 7:   Stop Listening To Vegetarians If You Want To Focus Better! 65

**Book 3:   Sugar and Your Body, Part 1
            Sugar and Health**

Chapter 8:   How Sugar Addiction May Be Ruining Your Health......................71

Chapter 9:   How Sugar Can Cause Insulin Resistance 75

Chapter 10: Is Sugar Giving You PMS...79

Chapter 11: Dump Sugar to Minimize Menopause Discomfort 83

Chapter 12: Has Fruit Addiction Simply Replaced Sugar Addiction? 87

Chapter 13: Salt's Okay? Sweet! (But Sugar Isn't....) 95

Chapter 14: Cholesterol: The Good, the Bad, and the Ugly 99

Chapter 15: Why Low-Carb Is Bad News 103

Book 4:   Sugar and Your Body, Part 2
**   Sugar & Weight Management**

Chapter 16: Calories In / Calories Out? Not Always. 109

Chapter 17: Alcohol Can Sabotage Your Weight Loss 115

Chapter 18: Size 6 or Size 4? 119

Chapter 19: Could Giving Sugar To Your Baby Make Her Fat? 123

Chapter 20: Sugar, Pregnancy, and Autism 127

Chapter 21: Can Dumping Kids' Sugary Diets Reverse Autism? 131

Book 5:   Sugar, Eating Behaviors and More

Chapter 22: Can Juvenile Delinquents and Broken Windows Help
             You Eat Less Sugar? (They Really Can!) 137

Chapter 23: A Standing Ovation For Throwing Away Sugar 141

Chapter 24: Always Have a Plan B: Stabilize Your Glucose
             (and Your Brain) On the Fly! 145

Chapter 25: Why Sugar Addiction and Raw Food Diets May Not Mix..........149

Chapter 26: Labeling Loopholes Help Sugar Sneak Into Your Food...............153

Book 6:   Recovery Rx:
Short-Term Cravings Elimination
Long-Term Plan For Conquering Sugar Addiction

Chapter 27: The Cravings Elimination Plan 159

Chapter 28: Stronger Than Sugar: Triumph Over Sugar Addiction...............163

Chapter 29: Your 7 Stability Steps..167

Chapter 30: What's Next?...171

INTRODUCTION

This book is dedicated to the millions of people just like you, who for years – even their entire lives – have struggled with sugar addiction and cravings. You haven't been taken seriously, and too often you've received misinformation on cravings ("Just think about something else!" "It's all in your head!").

I wrote this to let you know your sugar cravings are absolutely real, your addiction to sugar is absolutely real, and the solution is just as real.

It's based not on willpower, but on brain chemistry.

This book includes a "solution section." That's how-to stuff, and you will get it. You'll get short-term information on killing cravings right away, and a long-term plan for conquering sugar addiction permanently.

Even more, though, this is a "why-to" book. It's about your transformation, about becoming someone who is aware of the effects that sugar has on her brain chemistry, her appetite, her health, her moods, and her sense of self-efficacy. It's about becoming someone who **wants** to stay away from sugar for those reasons.

If you were looking for a book with recipes, shakes, products for sale, suggestions for ordering from restaurant menus, and substitute ingredients to let you keep eating a transmogrified version of your favorite cookies or cakes, then this book is not for you.

But if you care about the whys as much as the hows, and about what triumphing over sugar addiction can mean for you – inside, not just outside – then you will get the solution you seek, want, and need.

Thank you, and best wishes for your success in conquering sugar addiction, controlling (and ending) cravings, and transforming yourself so you can create the optimal health you deserve!

Joan Kent

SO WHO AM I, AND WHY SHOULD YOU LISTEN TO ME?

The short story is that I'm a sugar addict. I discovered that about myself a long time ago, decades before anyone knew about sugar's addictive effects. In fact, mentioning it to anyone was sure to result in a smirk, along with a "body scan," known these days as the up-and-down. I got tired of the smirks and the up-and-downs.

Back then, no one knew about sugar addiction or believed it to be true, so I had to fend for myself. And I eventually learned a lot.

Sugar addiction is based on brain chemistry and is often genetic. Because I had been adopted as an infant, I had no way of checking that out in my own family. I never met my birth parents (New York had closed adoption laws), and no one in my adoptive family seemed to have the same reaction to sugar that I noticed in myself.

I felt weird and somewhat ashamed. I tried to keep my sugar addiction a secret, but my family couldn't help but notice my preferences in food. Because they weren't a subtle bunch, they often made comments about the foods I liked. The comments were never kind.

In college, when I was eating on my own for the first time, my sugar situation got worse and kept getting worse when I was an adult. I can skip many of the details (lots of binges, frequent colds, many odd symptoms), except to tell you that I wanted sugar from the moment I woke up in the morning till I went to sleep at night. Sure, I ate other things, but only because I knew I was supposed to. All I ever really wanted was sugar. I don't think anyone ever wanted sugar more than I did.

My low point came when I left work one day at about 5:00 pm. It was summer and the sun was still shining. I had eaten some sugar a couple of hours earlier. As I drove on the freeway, I felt very tired and fell asleep behind the wheel. I woke up suddenly and had to brake hard to keep from hitting other cars. That made the car skid, turn ninety degrees, and slam into the left guardrail. The car was totaled. I was shaken, but relatively unhurt – although my neck was never quite the same after that.

Fortunately and miraculously, no other cars were involved in the accident. The police officer who arrived on the scene asked if I'd been drinking. I answered truthfully that I don't drink. That didn't stop him from shining a flashlight in my eyes and asking me to get out of the car to stand on one leg.

Well, I passed the drunk driving test, but we never discussed the subject of food. No one made those connections back then. Maybe that was fortunate for me in its own way, but the whole thing was, to say the least, a frightening experience and an extremely expensive lesson.

The Story Doesn't End There

In 1991 I met a woman who ran a treatment program for addicts. She used a unique system that kept the addicts on their recovery paths far more successfully than is usual in treatment programs. (Recidivism rates in addiction treatment tend to be extremely high.)

Until she met me, she didn't know that someone who was not an alcoholic or drug addict could be addicted to sugar.

I started going to all of her lectures and reading everything I could find on the subject of sugar addiction. That last part was really difficult. At that time, there was far less targeted material to read! It was a matter of piecing together everything I could find on the subjects of hypoglycemia, psychiatry, the neurochemistry of drug addiction and alcoholism, food cravings in addicts, brain chemicals affected by foods, and more.

After I'd spent a couple of years educating myself, the woman who ran the treatment center finally said the one thing I couldn't argue with: "Joan, this is all you think about, all you read about, all you talk about. Why don't you go back to school and do it for real?"

Until that moment, I had never thought about getting a Ph.D., but what she said made sense. It was a subject that fascinated me – and still does.

To cut to the chase, I got a doctorate in Psychoactive Nutrition – how foods affect neurochemistry (brain chemistry). Me, the woman who had always found classes in nutrition more boring than reading the phone book!

Okay, I still find most nutrition classes boring, but this particular doctoral program was about how foods affect behavior, eating behaviors, moods, cravings, food preferences, hormones, all kind of things. Great stuff, and far more interesting than the Food Guide Pyramid.

My dissertation involved using the information I'd been researching to treat women with binge-eating disorder. To shorten a four-year story, we found that sugar was a major trigger for both binge eating and cravings. Over the eight weeks of the pilot study, the low-sugar group got better results than either the low-fat group or the control group.

I was, to my knowledge, the first person to outline the neurochemical pathway of addiction to sugar (and also to saturated fat and white flour). That was in 1999. As you may know, the nutrition field has been moving in this neurochemical direction. Many people now acknowledge that sugar is an addictive substance, even a drug. Much information is available on how to quit sugar, end cravings, and more.

Interestingly, I have lately been subjected to a few self-titled nutrition "experts" who seem to be trying to discredit me. That's okay. Some of the information I use is based on drug addiction, which is what I studied at the time because that's what was available.

Could I go back and do the research again? Truth be told, as of this writing it's been over fifteen years, and I no longer have the time (or energy) it took to get my degree back then. I simply won't be studying at that level of intensity again. I *always* read and keep up with interesting updates, but mainly I listen to the wise voice of my late (and very great) mentor and coach. He used to remind me that I do what I do to help people. He reminded me that I have helped many people. And he told me to ignore my detractors and keep helping people.

The important thing is that for sugar addiction and cravings, *there is a treatment that works*. It's highly effective in getting people off sugar so they can improve their health, lose weight, feel better, and feel great about themselves.

So that's why I'm here. I recovered and so can you! I hope the information in this book helps you do that.

BOOK 1

THE BASICS OF SUGAR ADDICTION

CHAPTER 1
WHY SUGAR ADDICTION MATTERS

What good does it do to set goals for weight loss, better health, more energy, lower blood pressure, or lower cholesterol, when you can't reach those goals because your addiction to certain foods keeps sabotaging you? Has that happened to you?

Are you at risk for diabetes? For heart disease? Hypertension? Is your cholesterol too high?

Has your doctor told you to lose weight to reverse those conditions?

Have you been unable to follow your doctor's instructions because you can't stay away from your "trigger" foods?

Does it sometimes feel as if those forbidden foods are all you want to eat?

The foods you can't stop eating could be harming your health and more. The good news is that you're not alone. Food addictions are real. They're not psychological, emotional, or "mental." They're physiological.

With this new understanding, what would it mean to you to control your sugar intake?

How might your life change?

What would it be worth to have a proven system that changes not just how much sugar you eat, but how much you want it, and how you feel each day?

I've helped thousands of people conquer their addiction to sugar, stop craving it, and transform their health, mood, and weight. They feel more energetic, regain their willpower, shrink their appetite, change their eating behavior, and feel great about themselves for doing all of that.

I kicked sugar myself, but I didn't have this book. You do. My journey and my experiences can show you the way.

How much longer will you wait? Until you've gained more weight? Until your health suffers even more?

If you have kids, you want to be healthy enough to keep up with them when they're small, and still be around for the landmarks in their lives: graduations, weddings, job promotions, and even for your grandchildren, right? Of course you do.

How great would it be to become a healthy role model your children can be proud to follow? To show them what it's like to tackle a problem or a goal head-on and see it through to completion? What great lessons they could learn from your inner growth!

What about you? How do you want to feel about yourself – embarrassed to be at the mercy of sugar addiction, or proud to have solved one of the toughest problems in your life, *one that some people still say doesn't exist?* How great would it be to have self-control, self-esteem, and happiness?

If you're reading this book, you've probably decided that this sugar stuff has gone on long enough. Get started today! Use this book to put your plan into action. See how different life can feel when you're sugar free.

You're strong. You have it in you to be stronger than sugar. So start reading, learn about what's been going on with you, and follow my plan to *triumph over sugar addiction* once and for all.

Sugar Addiction Now Recognized As Mainstream Science

Good news! There's progress in the study of sugar addiction. For one thing, it's now acknowledged as real. (When I started doing this work, it wasn't – I remember how people would argue against the idea.)

I've known for decades that sugar addiction is based in neurochemistry, making it physiologically real. It's time that everyone recognized that.

Those who claim that sugar addiction is something else tend to be unaware of the physiology and neurochemistry of addiction, and also of the neurochemical effects of sugar.

Sugar addiction is still the most common food addiction I see in my practice.

Other common addictive foods, like saturated fats and processed white flour, are not always recognized as such, but they can be real addictions, too.

Genetic Factors May Predispose Someone to Sugar Addiction

The brain response to sugar can be as genetic as eye color. We each got what we got. Eye color is essentially permanent, but we can do something about our addiction to sugar.

Changing diet can change brain chemistry, cravings, appetite, mood, and food preferences – all in a good way. My doctoral dissertation was on the treatment of women with binge eating disorder. Eliminating sugar and adding the right foods significantly decreased binges and cravings.

To ignore someone's addictive response to sugar and treat it as if it were not an addiction helps no one. Treating it as an emotional problem misses the point and never gets to the underlying issue. (Amazingly, some people in the weight-loss field still do that.)

Even worse, it could make the addicted individual feel like a failure if she can't control her addictive response to sugar by treating it emotionally. How unnerving! The response is physiological, not a weakness or a lack of willpower.

In some ways, food addictions can be more difficult to conquer than other addictions. Obviously, abstinence is not an option. We can decide to give up alcohol or any other drug and only be the better for it, even if going through the rehabilitation is tough. But food is something we have to deal with several times a day, every day, for the rest of our lives, so the problem is insidious.

For someone who is susceptible, a number of foods can result in addiction. Sugar addiction seems to hinge on general, neurochemical responses that are common to all but become problematic for some due to predisposing factors. Those are based on family history.

Chapter 2 explains why and how sugar affects some people so strongly.

CHAPTER 2

WHY SUGAR ADDICTION AFFECTS SOME
OF US MORE THAN OTHERS

Have you ever noticed that some people react more strongly to sugar than others? They eat it more often, crave it frequently, and may want more even after they've eaten some.

Before we go further, let's talk about what we mean when we say 'sugar.' Sugar is a type of carbohydrate that's found in many foods. The most overt forms of sugar are things like cookies, candy, cakes and pastries. More covert sugars are the ones added to processed foods. Even "lightly" processed foods, such as dried cranberries, often contain sugar. To complete the list, we need to include syrups such as agave or maple syrup, dried fruit, fruit juice, fruit juice concentrate, and even fresh fruit. (More information on fruit in later chapters.)

The reasons for sugar addiction are often genetic. I love that. It takes any blame off the sugar addict and de-personalizes the reaction by making it chemical. We can't be blamed for something we didn't start, right? But we can still change it!

So what is this genetic, chemical thing that goes on in people who are susceptible to sugar addiction? It's in two parts – carbohydrate sensitivity and sugar sensitivity.

Carbohydrate Sensitivity

As explained above, sugar is a carbohydrate. Carb sensitivity is an exaggerated insulin release to sugar and some other carbs. Insulin facilitates the transfer of glucose out of the bloodstream, lowering your blood sugar level. Too much insulin can cause your blood glucose to drop too far and too fast. Your body responds by craving foods that will raise glucose quickly. Sugar is an obvious culprit in that regard.

The glucose drop can also trigger hunger, so it's likely that the carb-sensitive person will crave sugar, eat it, and eat quite a bit of it.

Who's likely to be carb sensitive? Typically, people with a family history of one or more of these: alcoholism, diabetes (including mature-onset), hypoglycemia, hypertension, or obesity. Another factor is central adiposity (apple-shaped body). The apple shape is characteristic of men, but women with that body type are more likely to be carb-sensitive.

Sugar Sensitivity

The other aspect – sugar sensitivity – is about brain chemistry. People who are sugar sensitive seem to have low baseline levels of endorphins (beta-endorphin), dopamine, and serotonin. To simplify (oversimplify!), these neurochemicals are linked to mood. The fact that these three chemicals are lower than normal makes sugar-sensitive people feel crummier than normal.

Who is likely to be sugar-sensitive? Typically, people with a family history of alcoholism, other addictions, depression or other mood disorders, or a personal history of PTSD (post-traumatic stress disorder).

What Happens When We Eat Sugar?

When we eat sugar, we get a brain release of endorphins (beta-endorphin). That triggers a dopamine response, because the two tend to go together. But when a sugar-sensitive person eats sugar, the endorphin release is greater than normal – and so is the dopamine.

Their serotonin will be exaggerated, too – because of carb sensitivity and high insulin release. It's linear. The more insulin we secrete, the more tryptophan (the amino acid used to make serotonin) travels to the brain, and the more serotonin we produce. Carb sensitives – who release extra insulin when they eat sugar – make a lot more serotonin after eating it.

What Does All of This Have to Do with Addiction?

Dopamine and endorphins (beta-endorphin) are involved in the reward part of sugar addiction. That means people who are sugar sensitive feel rotten without sugar, but *way better* than normal when they eat it. That effect reinforces and encourages repeat behavior.

Then there's serotonin. Serotonin is involved in seeking behavior – how much trouble we're willing to go through to get the addictive substance we want. Again, the exaggerated response comes in here. Extra insulin means extra serotonin and stronger seeking.

To recap, it works like this: A carb-sensitive, sugar-sensitive person feels crummy without sugar. The giant reward caused by extra-high dopamine and endorphins makes Ben & Jerry's seem irresistible in the middle of the night. Strong reinforcement after eating it provokes that desire on many nights. And extra serotonin makes her drive to the store in a bathrobe at 2:00 a.m. to get it.

The hormonal and neurochemical viewpoint is great because it takes all judgment off the person, who can't fight those genetics any more than we can fight our eye color. It leads to compassion, rather than judgment, for someone's compulsions. Judgment never helps anyone, although compassion can.

But, you might say, most people like a bit of sugar now and then. Some people even have a "sweet tooth," and we don't call them sugar addicts. So how can we distinguish a sweet tooth from sugar addiction? Let's take a look at that in Chapter 3.

CHAPTER 3
SUGAR ADDICTION OR SWEET TOOTH: WHAT'S THE DIFFERENCE?

Recently, a friend with a self-proclaimed sweet tooth asked me the difference between that and sugar addiction. The question brought out the geek in me, so I explored the difference. There is one.

Why We Like Sweet

Humans are hardwired to like sweet. In fact, a fetus will increase its swallowing of amniotic fluid if the fluid is artificially sweetened.

One author attributed our liking for sweet tastes to evolution. Millions of years ago we figured out that many plants that seem edible contain substances that can poison and even kill us quickly. Because that didn't happen with sweet foods, they became "safe."

Brain chemicals have a lot to do with liking sweet. Endorphins (beta-endorphin), dopamine, and serotonin are natural feel-goods that make us enjoy and want the sugary foods that trigger them.

So we like sweet stuff.

Some of us have a particular fondness for sweet foods – a sweet tooth – and may eat more of those foods than would be considered average (or healthful). People with a sweet tooth may show a preference for sweet foods whenever faced with a choice. They may even crave sugars at times.

Because of my background, I suspect there are neurochemical and/or hormonal reasons behind their preference for sweet, but let's just say for now that some people simply like sugar more than average.

Other people – and I shared in the intro that I was definitely one of them – go beyond *liking* sweet foods into having a *compulsion* to eat them. This may be a sign of an addiction to sugar.

Sugar Addiction Details

Addiction criteria apply very well to sugar addiction. Let's look at the section on Substance Abuse Disorder from the *Diagnostic and Statistical Manual of Mental Disorders, Fifth Edition* (DSM-5).

DSM-5 criteria for addiction are clustered in four groups, but are essentially the same as DSM-IV criteria. I've simply listed the criteria below, without the clusters. The examples given are just a few of many possible ones.

The severity of the disorder depends on the number of criteria present: two or three symptoms indicate mild, four or five indicate moderate, and six or more indicate severe substance abuse disorder. Some criteria may seem to apply only to illegal drugs, such as spending a great deal of time obtaining them. Sugar, of course, is available virtually everywhere, in unlimited quantities, and relatively inexpensively, but stay with me on this.

DSM-5 Criteria for Substance Abuse Disorder

1. Taking more of the substance, or for a longer period, than intended

Lack of control over what or how much one is eating characterizes binge-eating disorder. Chocoholics describe an inability to resist, moderate, or stop eating chocolate. Clients keep eating cake, one slice after another, despite planning to stop after one piece.

2. Unsuccessful efforts to stop or limit use

Dieting and weight cycling are found in binge eating and other eating disorders. Secret-eater chocoholics try unsuccessfully to reduce intake of chocolate, then relapse and overeat it.

3. A great deal of time spent obtaining, using, or recovering from use

Eighty percent of chocoholics state that chocolate interferes with their lives in some way. Purging behaviors might take increasing time. Excessive exercise, one example, could interfere with important activities or occur despite injury.

4. Craving the substance

Craving (an intense desire for a substance) is a common response to withdrawal or abstinence. Cravings are stronger after high levels of intake but can occur in other conditions. Cravings identify the substance that will relieve them – what you crave will take away the craving. (That's a poor way to deal with cravings, and the topic is covered in a later chapter.)

5. Failure to fulfill major obligations due to use

6. Continued used despite social problems caused or exacerbated by use

7. Giving up or reducing important activities because of substance use

Points 5-7 could show up as self-isolation; eating alone due to embarrassment over the eating; refusing to wear bright colors, form-fitting outfits, or swimsuits; refusing to attend social events, eat in public, be nude in front of others, make love with the lights on, look in the mirror, go to a gym with mirrors, or even go to a gym.

8. Recurrent use in hazardous situations

A client almost caused a car accident because she ran into a store to buy candy and "couldn't get the chocolate into (her) mouth fast enough." Hypoglycemia can also cause hazards, as I've described.

9. Continued use despite physical or psychological problems that are caused or exacerbated by substance use

Physical problems may include obesity, diabetes, hypertension, cardiovascular disease, and other illnesses. Chocoholics eat chocolate despite migraines or feeling sick.

10. Tolerance to effects of the substance (needing more to get the same effect)

Tolerance is reduced effectiveness of an addictive substance, so a larger dose is needed to obtain the same effect. Tolerance occurs with sweet substances. Both sugar and artificial sweeteners can change endorphin (beta-endorphin) function through up- or down-regulation.

Serotonin is another brain chemical that alleviates pain, and tolerance can occur to its effects as well. Serotonin production is higher when insulin release is higher, so more sugar means more serotonin, and may be the response to tolerance.

11. Withdrawal symptoms when not using or when using less

Withdrawal is a set of symptoms that addictive substances produce when chronic use stops or drops. It includes physical symptoms and negative moods, as specific brain chemicals decrease.

Eating more sugar or a food that contains sugar (like fruit) will relieve withdrawal symptoms.

Positive reinforcers *establish* addiction by causing pleasure. Negative reinforcers *alleviate* the pain or distress caused by the addiction. If sugar takes away the discomfort of withdrawal, the sugar is a negative reinforcer, even though it started as a positive reinforcer.

Most addictions end up being about negative reinforcement to stop withdrawal. The negative reinforcer can be either sugar itself or a substitute, but if it stops withdrawal symptoms, it has addictive potential. I'm thinking fruit, agave syrup, various sweeteners.

One withdrawal symptom is craving – an intense urge or desire for a substance. Cravings are highest when withdrawal is most severe, and the greater the intake, the greater the withdrawal and craving. (Chapter 5 is all about cravings.)

Among women, chocolate is the most craved food. Chocolate contains stimulants and mood elevators, including caffeine, theobromine (similar to caffeine), tyramine, and phenylethylamine (the being-in-love chemical).

Yet when chocolate isn't available, participants choose sweet substitutes, rather than stimulants like caffeine.

To that guy who loves to tell me that drug info doesn't apply to food:

Sugar isn't food; it's a drug.

Several journal articles, often by the same small group of researchers, "prove" sugar does nothing bad. In many cases, the sugar industry paid for the research. Enough said.

In the next section, we'll be looking at the interplay between sugar and the brain.

BOOK 2

SUGAR AND YOUR BRAIN

CHAPTER 4
WHY YOU SHOULDN'T EAT
WHAT YOU CRAVE

Back in 1998, I wrote a doctoral dissertation that investigated women with binge-eating disorder and their relationship with sugar. As I compared the DSM-IV criteria for substance dependence with the criteria for binge-eating disorder, it became obvious that addiction to sugar was most likely driving the binge eating. "No kidding," you say, but in 1998 this was radical thinking.

My research divided the participants, all screened for binge-eating disorder, into three groups.

The low-sugar group was given low-sugar nutrition guidelines to follow. They logged their food intake, including any binge episodes and/or cravings, and came to weekly support meetings.

The low-fat group followed low-fat guidelines, logged their food, binges, and cravings, and attended weekly meetings.

The control group had no nutrition guidelines or support meetings and simply logged their food, binges, and cravings.

All groups reported periodically for weigh-ins and measurements.

Bingeing and craving decreased most in the low-sugar group. Weight loss was greatest in that group, although the weight loss couldn't be fully explained by comparing calorie intake among the groups.

What I find funny (okay, maybe a little irritating) is that people are now, at long last, recognizing the connection between sugar addiction and the obesity epidemic.

I guess the 1985-1999 low-fat craze – and a "craze" it was – had to die out before people could see what was going on. (What can I say? My mother always told me I saw connections others didn't.)

The bad news is that sugar addiction is disturbingly and increasingly common, and may contribute significantly to obesity, diabetes, heart disease, and several types of cancer.

So How Does Sugar Contribute to the Obesity Epidemic?

- Sugar may trigger a "priming"-like reaction – a little can make us want more. This is due to a specific dopamine receptor in the brain. Some people experience this more acutely than others. I consider this effect of sugar the main argument *against* what's often suggested – to eat a small amount of what we crave. Priming can turn that into a very large amount.

- Sugar is addictive, so it definitely makes susceptible folks want lots of sugary food. It encourages over-consumption.

- Sugar addiction is physiologically real. It may cause withdrawal symptoms (cravings, agitation, restlessness, inability to focus, and more) when it's not available. Seeking and eating sugar to end the discomfort of withdrawal can lead to overeating and weight gain.

- Sugar may lead to something I call "secondary fat consumption." None of the study participants got cravings for fat; almost all got cravings for sugar. But in response to the sugar cravings, they'd often eat foods that contained lots of fat. For example, a craving for something sweet was likely to be answered with a bowl of ice cream, which is high in both sugar and fat.

Why? Research shows that fat makes sugar taste sweeter. The added calories due to the secondary fat consumption were significant in all groups.

- Sugar triggers the release of beta-endorphin (endorphins) in the brain. Beta-endorphin inhibits the brain's primary satiety center – the VMH (ventromedial hypothalamus). That can increase appetite, increase food consumption at a given meal, and lead to more frequent meals.

- Beta-endorphin changes food preferences and makes us want other endorphin triggers: fats or more sugar. The preference for healthful fare, such as vegetables, shrinks in comparison to those foods. Calorie intake can easily rise with high-sugar, high-fat foods.

Also, meals that are high in fat – including secondary fat – can trigger ghrelin, a hormone that tends to increase appetite as it slows metabolism. That's a potentially dangerous combination for weight and health.

It's clear from this list that sugar makes it all too easy to over-consume food and calories, especially empty calories. We can see the role it plays in binge eating and overweight. I stress that this connection was crystal clear to me in 1998 when I wrote my dissertation, and in 1999 when it was completed.

More than fifteen years later, others claim credit for this information; but it's actually old news. No one wanted to hear it then, but, fortunately, things have changed.

Since they seem to cause many problems, let's take a look at cravings, and see if we can destroy a few myths in the process.

CHAPTER 5

WHAT CAUSES SUGAR CRAVINGS?
(IT'S NOT WHAT YOU THINK!)

Cravings are a primary reason that sugar addicts may stay stuck – locked into their addiction. Understanding where cravings come from can help considerably in dealing with them.

Sugar Cravings Are Real

A food craving is an intense urge or desire to eat a specific type of food. One of the most common cravings is for sugary foods. Some people can indulge their sugar cravings without repercussions. For others, giving in repeatedly to cravings can undermine their fitness training or even lead to health issues – weight gain, high cholesterol, mood swings, diabetes, and more.

This chapter is about the origins of sugar cravings. In some cases, the origins discussed in this book are different from the ones you may have heard or read about in other places.

What We Usually Hear About Sugar Cravings

Mainstream Cravings Reason: Low Glucose

The cravings explanation we probably hear most often is the theory that low blood glucose is the cause of sugar cravings. Low glucose might occur if someone hasn't eaten in a long time, for instance, or has skipped breakfast and taken an early exercise class.

Evidence does support the low glucose theory. But there's more.

What's less known is that sugar cravings tend to occur in response to how *fast* glucose drops, rather than how *low*. So that could mean that someone was eating junky carbs. Junky carbs include sugar, processed flour, instant mashed potatoes, or other unhealthful foods. Those foods stimulate insulin production and are fast "glucose droppers."

When glucose drops because of high insulin release after eating junky carbs, it's called "reactive hypoglycemia."

Some people are carbohydrate sensitive. They release (secrete) more insulin than normal when they eat sucrose (table sugar). Carb sensitivity is documented in science journals and seems to be genetic.

Carbohydrate sensitivity is defined by the insulin response to sucrose, but sucrose is not the only carb that can cause high insulin release. Other junky carbs can, too, including fructose, the sugar found in fruit.

Not Your Usual Fructose Info

This is different from what you may hear about fructose: Some say it doesn't trigger insulin release. That statement is an oversimplification at best, and it doesn't apply to carb-sensitive people. Carb-sensitive folks do secrete insulin when they eat fruit, drink fruit juice, and so on.

As previously stated, "carb sensitives" tend to be people with a family history of hypertension, alcoholism, diabetes, or hypoglycemia. Having more than one of these genetic factors in the family (say, alcoholism on your father's side and diabetes on your mother's) could further increase the chances that you may secrete more insulin in response to certain carbs.

Fixing the Low-Glucose Theory

At the very least, let's add some information to the mainstream Low Glucose Theory of sugar cravings.

It's not just skipping a meal or going without food for a long time that may have caused your cravings. It might be that you ate some junky carbs, including fructose. If you're susceptible to carb sensitivity, that could have induced an exaggerated insulin response, leading to reactive hypoglycemia.

The fast drop of glucose in that situation can bring on cravings, typically for more sugar or other junky carbs. Your body knows that junk will bring up your glucose fast. Of course, it will drop again, but the body operates in the moment without reason or logic, so the craving can win.

Mainstream Cravings Reason: Emotions

Another commonly held view of cravings is that they're purely emotional.

In fact, some weight loss programs maintain that people who want to eat have two motives: Either they're physically hungry, or they're craving food for emotional reasons.

That's a bit too stark and "either/or" for me, especially since – as you'll discover – other reasons for cravings exist.

Let's start by agreeing that evidence does show that emotions can cause cravings. In science journals, a bad mood – any bad mood – is called "dysphoria." That's a fancy word for it, but any bad mood can bring on a sugar craving.

But we shouldn't overlook other reasons for cravings. One reason people crave sugar when they're in a bad mood is that sugar can bring mood "up."

Unfortunately, the effects of sugar on mood are only temporary. Besides, eating sugar will probably make things worse in the long run.

Fixing the Emotional Cravings Theory

So let's add another dimension to the Emotional Theory of Sugar Cravings. Emotions, especially bad ones, may indicate that a shift in brain chemistry has already occurred. As stated above, sugar can change mood. It changes brain chemistry in a way that alleviates the bad mood, even though it's only temporary and can bring on worse emotional states later.

What's tricky about it is this: That temporary improvement in emotional state is *reinforcing*. It makes us want to go back to sugar the next time emotions hit hard.

Please note that the *emotional* cravings reason is really a *brain* chemistry thing – and the programs that talk only about emotions and cravings miss that. We'll explore the brain chemistry of sugar cravings later in this chapter. This is key.

Mainstream Cravings Reason: Biological Need

Some sources think cravings express a biological need and should be answered by eating some of the craved food.

Salt cravings are usually the most common example given to corroborate this viewpoint. Some people crave salty foods after hard workouts, for example, which seems to suggest that salt cravings could indicate a biological need.

Yet evidence doesn't support this explanation with respect to sugar cravings. Sugar has been shown to be addictive. A drug addict will get cravings for a particular drug (heroin or cocaine, for example), and an alcoholic will get cravings for alcohol. But the cravings don't indicate a basic biological need. Obviously, we don't have a biological need for such things.

Salt is a mineral that the body needs. Sugar is just one type of carbohydrate, which we can get in many other, more healthful, forms.

Rejecting the Biological Need Theory

Cravings for sugary foods that have no true nutritional value don't indicate a basic biological need.

It's irresponsible to advise someone with strong or frequent sugar cravings to eat some sugar to stop the cravings. It could end up making the cravings worse. It could worsen the person's moods or result in mood swings. It could also harm her or his health if it's eaten often enough, especially in place of healthful foods. (That's what I used to do, and it wasn't good.)

So biological need doesn't apply to sugar cravings.

Let's look at some other possible causes of sugar cravings. I'll call them 7 **Real Cravings Reasons.**

Real Cravings Reason #1: Too Little Fat in Your Diet

In the science journals, you can find references to something called the sugar/fat seesaw.

As the name implies, the sugar/fat seesaw describes an inverse relationship in how much dietary fat and dietary sugar we eat. As one decreases in the diet, the other increases.

Fats stabilize blood glucose, so they can help us control sugar cravings.

But there are more important reasons to eat fats when trying to get rid of sugar cravings. When I was working on my Ph.D., there was no explanation for the sugar/fat seesaw in the science lit. In my dissertation, I offered the following explanation.

The Sugar/Fat Seesaw and Hormones

One part of the sugar/fat seesaw has to do with hormones. Different foods, or more specifically different nutrients in those foods, can play a role in hormone release. Here's how it works.

When fat enters the small intestine for digestion, a hormone called cholecystokinin (CCK) is released. CCK affects us by reducing hunger and appetite. It produces *satiety* – the feeling that we've had enough food and don't need to keep eating. Some of the behaviors that go along with satiety include reduced food intake, reduced carb intake, and even sleep.

On a very low-fat diet, CCK levels might be a lot lower. If CCK reduces intake of carbs (and of food in general), then low CCK could take away that feeling of satiety and make us want more food. Especially more carbs.

So it seems that low CCK from a very low-fat diet could contribute to a carb/fat seesaw.

But How Does Sugar Fit Into the Picture?

The second part of the sugar/fat seesaw has to do with a brain chemical already discussed, beta-endorphin (endorphins). Beta-endorphin is released when we eat sugar, fat, or both.

Endorphins belong to a family of brain chemicals called opioids. There's evidence that animals become accustomed to a given level of brain opioids. When the fat in their diets is decreased, they have a reaction that's described in research as "withdrawal."

Part of my hypothesis was: What if humans experience a similar reaction? If that were true, then sugar cravings could result from a diet that's too low in fats. (Remember, the nutrition field was anti-fat at that time!)

The *type* of fat matters, too. Animals given lots of saturated fats ate more protein and less carbohydrate than those that were on a diet low in saturated fats. This did not hold true when other types of fat – essential fatty acids, other polyunsaturated fats, or monounsaturated fats – were increased or decreased.

Why was that?

Researchers concluded that the mechanism of action was the difference in insulin secretion. Saturated fats promote insulin secretion; unsaturated fats don't. Insulin secretion can increase the brain's production (and release) of serotonin. The effect is pretty much linear: more insulin equals more serotonin.

Other research has shown that when serotonin levels go up, carbohydrate consumption drops. So serotonin seems to promote satiety for carbs. Serotonin can also increase satiety in general.

Because sugar boosts insulin release in a big way, it can enhance serotonin production (synthesis) and release in a big way. That linear effect is described above.

So if we don't get insulin and serotonin from saturated fats – especially if we cut back on sat fats because we've been told they're so bad for us – where will the serotonin come from?

Sugar. Sugar would provide two things: opioids to make up for the opioids the brain can't get in a low-fat diet, and lots of serotonin to make up for a lack of insulin-stimulating saturated fats.

Helpful Tip

While you're working on ending sugar cravings, don't worry about eating the "best" fats. Simply eat a little extra fat. I'm not telling you to junk out, but don't avoid fats for fear of the calories. Fats will help you give up sugar, even the ones you think you shouldn't eat – a little butter, for example, or cheese.

Real Cravings Reason #2: Withdrawal

When habitual use of addictive substances is interrupted, an "abstinence syndrome" can result. That's called withdrawal. Withdrawal can cause sugar cravings in a variety of situations.

If someone has recently stopped drinking alcohol, cravings for sugar can be strong and frequent. This involves the brain chemicals stimulated by alcohol. Alcohol stimulates three brain chemicals that are also stimulated by sugar.

The similarity makes sugar a short-term substitute for alcohol when cravings occur. It also explains why people in recovery from alcohol (or drugs) crave sugar, and may eat it often or in large quantities. Or both.

The phenomenon is so common that meetings of Alcoholics Anonymous (AA) often feature back-of-room treats that are laden with sugar: cookies, brownies, cakes, pastries. This approach can backfire, but we'll get to that in a moment.

If someone is addicted to sugar, quitting sugar can lead to cravings. The effect may be similar to the symptoms of alcohol withdrawal or opiate withdrawal – and also similar to the symptoms of hypoglycemia (low blood glucose).

(As a side note, I postulated years ago that hypoglycemia – especially reactive hypoglycemia, the rapid glucose drop following sugar ingestion in susceptible people – was a specific case of sugar withdrawal. Reviewing the lists below makes it seem a case can be made for that.)

Research shows that cravings are highest when withdrawal is most severe. The higher the level of intake prior to stopping, the greater the withdrawal and the subsequent craving.

Anyway, let's look at the symptoms in the three cases.

Alcohol Withdrawal Symptoms:	Hypoglycemia Symptoms:	Opiate Withdrawal Symptoms:
Sweating	Sweating	Sweating
Anxiety	Anxiety	Anxiety
Nausea	Nausea	Nausea
Irritability	Irritability	Agitation
Nervousness	Nervousness	Insomnia
Depression	Sadness	Goose bumps
Mood swings	Anger	Vomiting
Fatigue	Fatigue	Diarrhea
Shakiness	Shakiness	Abdominal cramping
Nightmares	Nightmares	Muscle aches
Clammy skin	Chills	Eye tearing
Headaches	Headaches	Runny nose
Confusion	Confusion	Yawning
Rapid heart beat	Rapid heart beat	Dilated pupils
Insomnia	Night sweats	Fever
Vomiting	Lightheadedness	
Pupil dilation	Dizziness	
Muscle tremor	Hunger	
	Sleepiness	
	Blurred vision	
	Tingling or numbness in lips or tongue	
	Weakness	
	Lack of coordination	
	Seizures	
	Unconsciousness	
	Difficulty speaking	
	Waking up tired, irritable or confused	

Research on lab animals that are made addicted to sugar shows withdrawal symptoms that resemble opiate withdrawal.

If you run a search on symptoms of sugar withdrawal, you'll find lists that include chills or sweating, especially at night; nausea and other gastric upsets; fatigue; low energy; mood swings; crankiness; headaches; hunger and the desire for sugary foods; muscle aches and pains; runny nose; yawning; insomnia.

Is sugar withdrawal just like withdrawal from opiates or alcohol? Some would say yes. Some would say that's too big a stretch. After all, the body has only so many ways of expressing itself, so a similarity in symptoms doesn't necessarily link them.

But we do know that, either directly or indirectly, sugar affects the same brain chemicals affected by alcohol and opiate drugs. Withdrawal may cause some similar symptoms in all three.

As mentioned previously, the similarity in affected neurochemicals makes sugar seem like a short-term substitute for alcohol.

Eating sugar when you crave either alcohol or sugar can backfire, however. It certainly doesn't stop the addiction, and it may lead to something known as priming.

Real Cravings Reason #3 deals with priming.

Real Cravings Reason #3: Triggers

Triggers may be external or internal. **External** triggers involve seeing or smelling an appealing food. These external triggers can prompt the desire for that food, in varying amounts.

Internal triggers involve eating a small amount of a trigger food. This type of triggering is known as "priming." A small amount of the food makes us want more. Priming is the result of a specific brain receptor for the chemical dopamine, the D2 receptor. Some people are more susceptible to priming than others.

Eating a bit of the food we crave is offered up as mainstream "wisdom." Unfortunately, that "wisdom" to eat what you crave can be terrible advice for a sugar addict. Sugar addicts are very sensitive to priming. As stated in an earlier chapter, priming is probably the best argument *not* to eat what you crave, since it's likely to start a binge.

To illustrate, let's look at something besides food. Some people can have half a glass of wine, shrug their shoulders, and have no desire for more till the next holiday season. But those who are susceptible to priming might have half a glass of wine and decide to finish the bottle singlehandedly. Worse, they might even go on a drinking binge for several days.

Since this book is not intended to cover addiction to alcohol or drugs, let's return to sugar.

A similar response can happen with sugar. Sugar has been shown to stimulate a release of beta-endorphin (endorphin, the same chemical that causes the runner's high). Beta-endorphin in turn stimulates a release of dopamine. When the D2 dopamine receptor binds with dopamine, people who are susceptible to priming may want more sugar and crave it.

Some people insist priming doesn't apply to food, just to alcohol or drugs. But animal studies (don't run away yet!) suggest that animals treat alcohol as an alternative food and consume it for the characteristics it shares with sugar (namely, its effect on brain chemicals). By inference, priming may apply to sugar, as well.

Decades of clinical experience show that priming does apply to sugars, and that avoiding possible priming goes a long way toward ending cravings. My advice would be to take priming seriously if you're serious about ending sugar cravings.

Because of the priming-type effect, quitting sugar "cold turkey" is often the best way to go.

Not everyone wants to hear that! It's understandable. After years of sugar addiction, you're reluctant to let it go.

But trying to wean yourself from sugar bit by bit can make it impossible to quit because priming provokes the desire for more sugar. And a little bit can cause big cravings.

If there were a way you could eliminate sugar cravings and quit without stress or struggle, wouldn't it be worth it?

•   Sugar would be out of your diet.

•   The repercussions of eating sugar, covered in a later chapter, would be out of your life.

•   You could potentially, and finally, reach the health you've always wanted – reducing weight, eliminating heart disease, lowering blood pressure, lowering cholesterol, lowering triglycerides, reversing diabetes, and more.

•   If you're pregnant, or planning to be, your improved metabolic health could potentially reduce the risk that your child will develop autism spectrum disorders. (More on this important point in Chapter 20.)

Being healthy enough to stick around and be there for your family is a compelling reason to kick sugar cravings, kick sugar, and get your food on track.

Don't be tempted by a small bite of cake or half a cookie. Wanting more isn't worth the tiny taste. Find foods containing sugar by reading labels. Then avoid them. That doesn't mean you can't eat anything with sugar ever again. But avoiding it now will help you eliminate it so it loses control over you.

An easy and complete plan for conquering sugar addiction is in Book 6.

Real Cravings Reason #4: Stress

Okay, it's mean for sure. When researchers want to stress mice, they pinch their tails. The first thing the mice do? Run to their food bowls and eat. It's an endorphin (beta-endorphin) thing. Beta-endorphin is released in response to either pleasure or pain / distress. And endorphins increase appetite.

Have your friends ever complained about gaining weight when they're stressed? Did you believe them? Did you think they were just trying to avoid taking responsibility for eating high-calorie foods?

Well, when the stressed mice are given a choice between ordinary mouse chow and crumbled cookies, which do you think they choose? Yes, cookies – another endorphin thing. Release of endorphins makes sugar and fat more appealing.

So, since stressed mice do what we do under the same circumstances, maybe we can be kind to ourselves when we do it.

Of course, with people it's more complex. Some are highly susceptible to beta-endorphin and may react to stress by eating. For others, though, short-term stress decreases appetite. An important early morning presentation at work could bring on a stress-chemical cascade that leads to skipping breakfast.

Once that presentation is done, a different hormone – cortisol – takes over and *increases* appetite. Lunch that day might make up for the skipped breakfast, and then some.

Long-Term Stress Is Different

In long-term stress, cortisol plays a more prominent role. It keeps stimulating appetite. It decreases serotonin, and that can cause anxiety or depression. Those bad moods in turn can cause cravings –

mostly for carbs and, of course, not for healthful ones.

The low serotonin also reduces satiety (the feeling we've had enough food) – especially for carbs – and makes us more impulsive. That interesting combination makes it more likely that we'll eat the junky carbs we're craving.

Over the long term, high cortisol also decreases two other brain chemicals: dopamine and norepinephrine. When serotonin, dopamine, and norepinephrine drop, that leads to cravings, addictions, impulsive and compulsive behaviors, and a preference for carbs and sugars.

Over time, cortisol decreases endorphins (beta-endorphin). Chronically low beta-endorphin increases addictive or compulsive behaviors, including alcoholism, bulimia, binge eating, and more.

Metabolic and Health Effects of Stress

None of this even touches on the metabolic problems cortisol causes. For one thing, fat deposits in the trunk of the body, which is the more harmful location. Too much cortisol can bring on glucose disturbances and even insulin resistance.

Insulin resistance can lead to type 2 diabetes, high blood pressure, high triglycerides, low HDL (good) cholesterol, and high or dense LDL. LDL is usually called "bad cholesterol," and it's worse when it's dense. Insulin resistance also causes plaque formation in the arteries, heart disease, various cancers, and more.

Obviously, long-term stress leads to serious consequences in health, metabolism, and appetite. So while it might not be our fault for eating cookies, health-wise, it's far from ideal.

It's understandable that a stressed-out person might want a martini or a dish of chocolate ice cream. The point is, giving in will probably backfire. Stress depletes B vitamins, which are critical in the formation of key brain chemicals. (More on the critically important B vitamins later in this chapter.)

Alcohol – the go-to stress-reliever for some people – also destroys B vitamins and makes it more difficult to stabilize brain chemicals. So even though avoiding alcohol may feel tough to do when you're under stress, it can actually help more than drinking will.

In addition, long-term alcohol or sugar use will eventually decrease serotonin and beta-endorphin, resulting in rotten moods and major cravings. That means staying away from sugar can help, too.

We'll cover getting away from sugar soon, but right now, let's keep looking at causes of cravings. Serotonin is a fascinating brain chemical that has profound affects on cravings, appetite, and food preferences.

Real Cravings Reason #5 is about how serotonin affects what we want to eat.

Real Cravings Reason #5: Problems With Serotonin

Serotonin is an important brain chemical that has become commonly known due to several anti-depressant medications that have been on the market for years. Disturbances in serotonin may include depression, seasonal affective disorder (SAD), premenstrual syndrome (PMS), menopause, chronic alcohol use, or insulin resistance. Any of these can lead to sugar cravings.

PMS includes a long list of symptoms and signs: anxiety, depression, irritability, mood swings, nervousness, angry outbursts, fatigue, fluid retention, bloating, weight gain, backache, cramps, headaches, joint pain, breast pain, insomnia, acne, and cravings. Whew!

Factors that contribute to PMS include hormonal changes, neurochemical shifts, stress, diet, and lack of exercise.

Serotonin is one brain chemical associated with PMS. Another is beta-endorphin. Premenstrually, both chemicals drop – with interesting effects.

Serotonin promotes relaxation, calm and satiety (the feeling we've had enough food). It can reduce depression, stress, anxiety, and pain. During PMS, the drop in serotonin may lead to irritability, pain, depression, mood swings, impulsivity, increased appetite – and cravings, especially for carbs.

Diet Can Affect Serotonin

Poor diet can be a big reason that someone might suffer from low serotonin. Diets that are too low in starches (this happens a lot now that people have become anti-"carb") can cause serotonin to drop. More on this in Chapter 15.

Poor diet can also cause PMS symptoms. Women with PMS tend to have higher intakes of sugar, alcohol, white flour, salt, saturated fat, caffeine, and dairy products.

At the same time, women with PMS tend to eat diets that are low in B vitamins, protein, essential fatty acids, and fiber. Eating more of those items can alleviate symptoms, so the combination of low intake of these foods and high intake of the foods in the previous paragraph may be problematic.

Let's focus on high sugar intake. Sugar worsens the intensity of PMS symptoms. It increases breast tenderness, congestion and pain; abdominal bloating; and swelling of the face and extremities. Sugar also increases magnesium excretion, which in turn can result in irritability, anxiety, depression, low brain-reward chemicals, and insomnia.

Any of these symptoms can bring on sugar cravings. It's a self-perpetuating cycle.

Another factor that interferes with serotonin is insulin resistance. Insulin resistance can cause sugar cravings and even depression. Let's see how this works.

Insulin Resistance and Serotonin

Insulin is a hormone that's produced by the pancreas and facilitates the transfer of glucose from the bloodstream to the cells. (It has several other functions, as well.)

Under certain circumstances, someone might become *insulin resistant*. The cells no longer respond to insulin's cues, and consequently don't accept enough glucose. To get more glucose into the cells, the body's first line of defense is to produce more insulin. This may work, and can continue to work until the production of insulin no longer outpaces the degree of resistance. (That's an extremely oversimplified description of the onset of type 2 diabetes.)

Meanwhile, these high levels of insulin are not harmless and are likely to cause a variety of health issues. The issues may include heart disease, type 2 diabetes, hypertension, cholesterol problems, certain cancers, and more.

It's not insulin resistance per se that causes those diseases, but the extra insulin that's released to compensate when the body becomes resistant. This extra insulin is associated with inflammatory hormones called Series 2 prostaglandins. (More on prostaglandins in Chapter 8.)

What we typically hear about insulin resistance is that it's caused by obesity. That's true, but it's not the whole picture. Insulin resistance can be caused by genetics or by lifestyle, including lack of exercise and/or poor diet.

So what does all of this have to do with sugar cravings?

The primary site of insulin resistance is skeletal muscle. How does insulin-resistant muscle behave? It doesn't allow glucose to enter the muscle cells. The glucose ends up being transported to fat cells. And cravings for carbs, specifically sugar, can result.

An interesting connection with depression exists, too, leading to more cravings.

You may recall from seventh-grade biology that amino acids are the building blocks of protein. Insulin helps transport amino acids to muscles, where they're used for a variety of functions: formation of blood, hormones and enzymes; wound healing and tissue repair; energy use; and lots more.

A top-priority function is the making of specific brain chemicals from specific amino acids. The amino acid tryptophan is the one the brain uses to make serotonin.

Insulin resistance can interfere with tryptophan's transport to the brain. That can lower serotonin production. Low serotonin is linked with depression, and, like any bad mood, depression can trigger cravings. Sugar cravings are common.

The next Real Cravings Reason looks at how protein can affect sugar cravings. This is major.

Real Cravings Reason #6: Too Little Protein in Your Diet

Eating too little protein can be a huge cause of sugar cravings. Vegetarians may experience this. In my clinical experience, vegans (who eat no animal products at all) frequently have extremely strong cravings for carbs – most often for sugar.

Sugar cravings have a lot to do with brain chemicals. Quitting successfully requires building up those chemicals so they benefit you.

As stated above, protein is made of amino acids – the building blocks of protein. Amino acids build the brain chemicals we need – dopamine, serotonin and others. When those chemicals are at optimal levels, we don't crave sugar, we think clearly, and we resist cravings more easily.

So we need protein to make the brain chemicals that stop sugar cravings.

What About Hormones?

Let's look at the hormone we discussed earlier – CCK. Protein is another nutrient (along with fat, as you may recall) that promotes a release of CCK as it enters the small intestine for digestion.

Between the drop in CCK and the decreased brain chemicals caused by a low-protein diet, strong cravings for carbs like sugar can result.

Once again, endorphins (beta-endorphin) may play a role. Most animal protein also contains fat. The beta-endorphin released in response to the fat in a high-protein meal helps to keep sugar cravings under control – or even eliminate them.

Protein foods include poultry, fish, lean beef, lamb, pork, eggs, shellfish, cottage cheese, and Greek yogurt with 18 to 20 grams of protein per serving.

I'm a Vegetarian (or Vegan). What Kind of Protein Should I Eat?

If you're vegan and crave sugar often, it can help to eat some animal protein in whatever form you're willing to eat it. Some vegan clients of mine who experienced severe sugar cravings were willing to eat eggs, fish, or shrimp.

Some were willing to eat high-protein yogurt. A yogurt with 18 to 20 grams of protein in a serving is high-protein. (Less will not be enough, especially if the yogurt is flavored, which usually means sweetened.)

If you're absolutely unwilling to eat animal protein, eggs, or dairy, it may be necessary to use vegetable protein powders. Make sure the protein powder is unsweetened. This can be a highly effective option, and I use it frequently.

Make no mistake: adequate protein is key to eliminating sugar cravings.

Some people eat nuts, thinking they're protein. But nuts are primarily fats – good fats, yes, but they contain very little protein. Nuts, especially raw, are good to include in your diet, but you'd have to consume a lot of fat to get a small amount of protein from them.

In a later chapter, you'll discover the protein imposters – foods that are *considered* protein, but really aren't. Don't settle.

Never skimp on protein when you're trying to cut out sugar cravings or conquer your sugar addiction. More info on protein is in Chapters 6 and 7.

B vitamins play a significant role in controlling sugar cravings. Let's take a look at those.

Real Cravings Reason #7: B Vitamin Deficiencies

"B" is definitely for "Brain" – and B vitamins are another key in wiping out sugar cravings.

B vitamins play an important role in several brain functions. Here are some of those functions and lists of foods that contain the specific vitamin. A deficiency in one B vitamin is possible, but, as a rule, the deficiencies tend to occur in clusters.

Thiamin

Thiamin deficiency can change serotonin function and sleep patterns. Thiamin deficiency may also cause behaviors associated with depression, and has been linked with the dysfunction of two other brain chemicals – dopamine and norepinephrine.

Good sources of thiamin include organ meats, pork, peas, beans, and unrefined grains. Deficiency can be caused by carb-heavy diets of refined foods (sugar, white flour, white rice).

Niacin

Niacin deficiency results in pellagra, associated with dementia, as well as dermatitis and diarrhea. Niacin can be made from dietary tryptophan, an amino acid. Since protein-containing foods are major sources of both niacin and tryptophan, a low-protein diet could be a cause of niacin deficiency. Nuts and legumes are other sources of niacin.

Vitamin B6

B6 plays a significant role in brain chemical function.

The conversion of tryptophan to serotonin depends on B6. Low B6 may be linked with low serotonin levels, particularly in women, who have higher turnover rates of brain serotonin than men.

PMS is associated with low serotonin. The most common type of PMS involves anxiety, irritability, and nervous tension. It's found in women who consume excessive refined sugar and dairy products, both poor sources of B6. This type of PMS responds well to B6.

B6 deficiency is associated with psychological distress, depression, fatigue, and confusion. Since B6 is necessary for the synthesis of serotonin, lower serotonin due to B6 deficiency is considered a primary factor. Administration of B6 has been shown to decrease psychological distress.

Because melatonin is synthesized from serotonin, B6 deficiency may also reduce melatonin production. Reduced melatonin, the "sleep hormone" and an important anti-inflammatory, may disturb sleep patterns and increase inflammation. More on inflammation in a later chapter.

B6 is also important in the production of dopamine, norepinephrine, GABA, and other neurochemicals. Low levels of dopamine and norepinephrine are associated, respectively, with lack of pleasure (anhedonia) and depression.

Processed grains lose considerable B6. Alcohol destroys B6 and reduces serotonin.

The richest sources of B6 tend to be chicken, fish, kidney, liver, pork, and eggs. Other good sources include lima beans, brown rice, whole grains, soy, peanuts, walnuts, avocados, and vegetables.

Folate

Folate deficiency occurs often in depression, and folate often reverses depressive symptoms. Low folate has been linked with poor response to certain antidepressants (SSRIs).

Alcohol consumption causes folate malabsorption. All folate is lost from refined foods, such as sugars.

Good sources of folate are beef, lamb, pork, chicken liver, eggs, salmon, and green leafy vegetables.

As you can see, B vitamins are often found in protein foods, so keeping the protein content of your diet high can help maintain levels of several B vitamins and control cravings. In the next two chapters, you'll discover additional reasons that protein is so important.

CHAPTER 6

ARE YOU EATING THESE PROTEIN IMPOSTERS?

Protein is the key nutrient for trampling sugar cravings. Don't be fooled by these protein imposters.

Protein Imposter #1: Nuts and peanut butter
Nuts contain good, healthful fats. Monounsaturated, mostly. It's good to eat them, but don't consider them a protein source. There's not enough protein in them to earn that label! Peanut butter, actually a legume, is a hotly debated food, but it too is mostly monounsaturated fat (plus a little saturated fat), rather than protein.

Protein Imposter #2: Yogurt
Okay, some yogurt has enough protein to count as a protein food. Be sure you select one of those brands: Fage, Chobani, Trader Joe's Greek-Style Yogurt. For each brand, select the unflavored type.

Beware: These brands now make so many different varieties – some absolutely loaded with added sugar – that you need to choose with care. The sweetened ones can make it impossible to stop your sugar addiction.

Protein Imposter #3: Quinoa
Quinoa is a carbohydrate! Treat it as one. Have a moderate portion (it's quite nutritious), but eat real protein with it (fish, chicken, eggs, grass-fed beef, protein powder).

What Difference Does It Make?

Why does it matter whether your food is real protein or an imposter? For one thing, protein has many functions in the body. And when it comes to ending sugar addiction, protein helps.

Here are some benefits of protein, some discussed in previous chapters:

• Protein promotes CCK, as described in earlier chapters. CCK (cholecystokinin) is a powerful hormone that makes us feel full and turns off the desire for carbs. Vegetarians often have intense cravings for sugar and other carbs because they don't get enough protein, or because they eat protein imposters instead.

• Proteins are made of amino acids, which we learned are the "building blocks of protein." Protein contains the amino acids that the brain uses to make the key chemicals that keep our brains functioning optimally so we don't crave junk. If you're trying to give up sugar, protein is critical for killing sugar cravings.

• Protein improves mood. It helps the brain make chemicals that keep us awake and feeling great (dopamine and norepinephrine). Protein also provides the B vitamins (thiamin, niacin, B6, folate) that are catalysts in the creation of those important brain chemicals. Many food plans underplay protein, which may reflect under-emphasis (or lack of awareness) of protein's effects on brain chemistry.

- Protein foods are the only ones that stimulate the release of glucagon. The hormone glucagon opposes the effects of insulin (which, among other things, promotes fat storage). Glucagon is typically released when we exercise and when we eat protein. It can help boost metabolism, decrease cholesterol production, block the growth of arterial smooth muscle cells to prevent increased blood pressure, and more.

High-protein foods include fish, poultry, beef, lamb, shrimp, crab, eggs, cottage cheese, unsweetened protein powder, and the right type of yogurt (see above).

Other foods do contain some protein, but a food that contains a little protein isn't necessarily a protein food. Almost every food is a combination of protein, carb, and fat – or at least two out of the three.

Quinoa illustrates this mistake perfectly. Frequently praised for its protein content, it's really 70% carb, with the remaining calories equally divided between protein and fat. As healthful as quinoa is, a food with those nutrient ratios has a completely different effect on brain chemistry and hormones than a food high in protein.

Never skimp on protein if you want to trample those sugar cravings.

Protein also helps us focus. Let's take a look at that next.

CHAPTER 7

STOP LISTENING TO VEGETARIANS IF YOU WANT TO FOCUS BETTER!

True observation: Quite a few participants in my athletic training program were unable to focus for more than thirty seconds at a time. No exaggeration. It was particularly noticeable in rowing. (It's easier to hide on a bike.)

The problem seemed to correlate with the fact that they were vegetarians.

Another rowing instructor told me that someone in his class "couldn't focus longer than thirty seconds." When I asked, it turned out the man in question was a vegetarian.

Yes, I realize not every vegetarian lacks focus. However, the rowers who couldn't stick with the training for more than thirty seconds were invariably vegetarians.

The advice I gave to my participants (and suggested the other instructor give to his) was to increase protein. This has to mean "real" protein, so the tricky part is finding an acceptable form of protein that a vegetarian is willing to eat.

When I explained to one participant the brain chemistry of protein and how it affects focus, he was willing to add fish and shrimp to his diet. Within a few days, things had turned around, and he had no difficulty focusing on the rowing workout. Presumably, his focus improved in other areas, too.

Which brings me to that vegetarian beans-and-rice thing.

You've probably heard it. Beans and rice are an oft-touted vegetarian meal that is said to provide complete protein. For those who are unfamiliar with the idea of complete proteins, it has to do with the amino acids of which proteins are made.

When we eat animal proteins – fish, poultry, grass-fed beef, eggs, yogurt with eighteen-plus grams of protein per serving – we get all the amino acids necessary for human metabolic function.

When we eat non-animal sources of protein, some amino acids are missing from the foods. Other foods must provide the missing amino acids to complete the spectrum.

Neither rice nor beans contain much protein; both foods are primarily starch (carbohydrate). So, beans and rice together do provide the complete list of amino acids, but they give us only a small amount of protein overall. Lots of starch, though. The effect of starch on brain chemistry is completely different from that of protein.

As mentioned in a previous chapter, complete protein increases production of dopamine and norepinephrine by providing tyrosine and phenylalanine, the amino acid precursors. Dopamine and norepinephrine are alertness and focus chemicals. Carbs tend to raise serotonin levels, which make us relaxed, drowsy, and even "spacey."

Vegetarians no longer suggest combining proteins at a given meal; that recommendation is long outdated. But ignoring it can make things even worse for someone who tends to lose focus without animal protein.

It's not my place to tell vegetarians to stop being vegetarians. And I wish vegetarians would stop calling rice and beans protein foods.

If you have trouble focusing – I wonder if people who have the problem even know it – a good recommendation might be to add some form of animal protein to your diet.

If that's out of the question (obviously, people are vegetarians for different reasons), at least add a serving of high-quality vegetable protein powder to every meal to provide a full protein serving with the complete amino acid spectrum.

Incidentally, vegans often have screaming cravings for sugar, and again the answer starts with protein. Cravings are so often a brain chemical thing.

For vegans with sugar cravings, unsweetened vegetable protein powder might be the most important part of a permanent solution for defeating sugar addiction.

In Book 3, we'll look at the significant effects of sugar on our health.

BOOK 3

SUGAR AND YOUR BODY, PART 1

SUGAR & HEALTH

CHAPTER 8

HOW SUGAR ADDICTION MAY BE RUINING YOUR HEALTH

We know our health matters. Probably everyone agrees that what we eat affects our health. Nutrition approaches to health vary widely. Some people focus on organic foods, some on raw foods, others on herbs, phytonutrients and colorful pigments. There are low-carb, macrobiotic, and Ayurvedic diets, and many more.

One key, often overlooked, health factor is the production of **prostaglandins**. Prostaglandins are short-lived, hormone-like chemicals that are produced within cells and move from cell to cell, rather than through the bloodstream. They regulate all kinds of cellular activities.

Prostaglandins and Inflammation

Inflammation has become a hot topic in medicine. More and more research indicates that most disease begins with inflammation, and it's a highly complex topic.

Many causes of inflammation are beyond the scope of this book. One source of inflammation that ties in with sugar consumption is a specific prostaglandin. Foods, and certainly sugar, can influence prostaglandin production.

Following are the three prostaglandin types and a greatly simplified explanation.

Series 1 prostaglandins control factors that we recognize as beneficial. They dilate blood vessels, reduce blood pressure, inhibit unnecessary clotting, decrease autoimmune disease risk, improve T-cell function, improve insulin sensitivity, decrease pain, decrease inflammation, decrease the need for sleep, and alleviate depression. They also do much, much more.

Series 1 are made from dietary fatty acids in the omega-6 category. These include black current seed, flaxseed, hemp seed, pumpkin seed, walnuts, borage oil, evening primrose oil, sesame oil, sunflower oil, and more.

Series 2 prostaglandins do basically the opposite of the Series 1 functions listed above, as well as those not listed. Series 2 prostaglandins *promote* pain and inflammation, making them a prime culprit in disease.

Series 2 are also made from omega-6 fatty acids. However, high insulin secretion causes a different enzyme to act on the omega-6 fats, resulting in production of Series 2, rather than Series 1.

As previously stated, major insulin triggers include sugars, processed carbs (like white bread), saturated fats, alcohol, and others.

Series 3 prostaglandins reduce the negative effects of Series 2. They decrease inflammation and enhance immune function. Series 3 are made from omega-3 fatty acids, which we often hear about these days because they have anti-inflammatory benefits. So they can help reduce what's presently considered the cause of most disease.

Omega-3 fatty acids include dark green leafy vegetables, fish oils, seeds (black currant, flax, hemp, and pumpkin) and walnuts.

Because sugar and other addictive foods can cause inflammation – currently considered the primary root of health risks – ending your sugar addiction can reduce inflammation and improve your health.

No matter how stuck you feel now, sugar doesn't have to be part of your future.

My 7 Stability Steps in Book 6 are designed specifically to help you triumph over sugar addiction, trample cravings, and transform your health in exactly the ways we covered in this chapter.

CHAPTER 9

HOW SUGAR CAN CAUSE INSULIN RESISTANCE

Type 2 diabetes is epidemic in this country, and typically begins with insulin resistance.

What we usually read or hear about insulin resistance is that it's a result of obesity or overweight. That's true but not always the case; the reverse can also occur.

Insulin resistance may actually *cause* an increase in weight.

What's important is this: No matter which comes first – insulin resistance or overweight – the metabolic consequences are exactly the same.

Dietary sugar and fructose can play a role in causing insulin resistance, and that can happen in several ways. Insulin resistance appears to result from changes in both receptor *number* and receptor *activity* or *sensitivity.*

Where Does Food Fit in the Picture?

A high-carbohydrate diet can lead to insulin resistance, particularly if the carbs are high on the glycemic index (GI). Sugar would be a prime example of a high-GI carb. High-glycemic carbs are quickly absorbed and trigger a high insulin response. (The glycemic index is flawed for several reasons and is mentioned here *only* because it can help pinpoint highly insulin-triggering carbs.)

The high levels of insulin secretion can, in turn, lead to a diminished response by the body to insulin. This is due to something known as *down-regulation.*

Down-regulation is a term originally borrowed from brain chemistry research. It refers to a reduction in both the *number* of insulin receptors and the *sensitivity* of the receptors. The changes mean that insulin no longer works as well as it did before.

Down-regulation is more likely to occur in someone who is carbohydrate sensitive, with an exaggerated insulin response to sucrose or other carbs. That extra high insulin release is also more likely to down-regulate insulin receptors because of the body's bias toward homeostasis. Down-regulation of insulin receptors occurs fairly rapidly.

So eating sugar – especially lots of sugar, as might occur with sugar addiction – can cause insulin resistance.

What About Fructose?

There's a rather odd adaptation here. Fructose has been shown to change muscle fibers from type 1 to type 2b. Type 1 is a high-endurance fiber that responds well to insulin, while Type 2b is better for explosive power but is less responsive to insulin.

It's a well-known fact that fructose triggers insulin resistance. Research suggests that this muscle fiber change is the mechanism behind that. Even though the original research was done on animals, studies on human subjects have shown similar results. Athletic training can modify the results somewhat.

The bottom line is that fructose – which is half of the sucrose molecule – may cause insulin resistance in this interesting way.

It could even be said that sucrose (granulated table sugar) might cause insulin resistance through two mechanisms: down-regulation of insulin receptors *and* modified muscle fiber type due to the fructose in it.

How much more true might this be if sugar were eaten in large quantities – say, by sugar addicts?

All research seems to confirm that the fructose in sucrose is what makes sucrose the junk that it is.

Health recommendations? Skip the sugar. Definitely skip processed fructose or concentrated fruit juice used as a sweetener. Get your wholesome nutrients primarily from vegetables and only incidentally from fruit.

This isn't what you'll hear most places, but it may be more effective than what you'll hear elsewhere. More complete nutrition recovery information is coming up in Chapter 29.

In the meantime, let's look at how sugar can affect PMS symptoms.

CHAPTER 10

IS SUGAR GIVING YOU PMS?

Diet may not be the only reason you suffer from premenstrual syndrome, but it could be a big one.

PMS includes a long list of symptoms and signs. To recap, they include anxiety, depression, irritability, mood swings, nervousness, angry outbursts, fatigue, fluid retention, bloating, weight gain, backache, cramps, headaches, joint pain, breast pain, insomnia, acne, and cravings.

Factors that contribute to PMS include hormone or neurochemical shifts, diet deficiencies, stress, and lack of exercise.

Two important brain chemicals associated with PMS are serotonin and beta-endorphin (endorphins). Premenstrually, both chemicals drop, with interesting effects.

What Happens When Those Chemicals Drop?

Serotonin promotes relaxation, calm and satiety – the feeling that we've had enough food. It can reduce depression, stress, anxiety, and pain. During PMS, the drop in serotonin can lead to irritability, pain, depression, mood swings, impulsivity, increased appetite – and cravings, especially for carbs.

Beta-endorphin reduces pain and emotional distress, while it promotes wellbeing, euphoria, and sensations of reward in the brain. When beta-endorphin drops during PMS, we feel more pain, have low moods, and get cravings, especially for sugars and fats.

Serotonin and beta-endorphin are strongly influenced by diet and exercise. How does repeated sugar consumption affect this?

As described in Chapter 5, women with PMS tend to have high intakes of sugar, alcohol, white flour, salt, saturated fat, caffeine, and dairy products. From the other side, PMS is linked with low levels of B vitamins, protein, essential fatty acids, and fiber. These dietary habits tend to be either/or. One cancels out the other.

Let's Focus on High Sugar Intake

As explained earlier, sugar increases the intensity of PMS symptoms: breast tenderness, congestion and pain; abdominal bloating; and swelling of the face and extremities. Sugar increases magnesium excretion, which results in irritability, anxiety, depression, low brain reward, and insomnia.

Sugar triggers high insulin secretion. Insulin affects hormones known as prostaglandins (as explained in Chapter 8) and increases Series 2, the ones that cause pain and inflammation.

Sugar increases appetite for junk food, cravings, and hypoglycemia in people who are susceptible. Alcohol does these things, too, and can decrease serotonin besides. Not a good mix of effects from either of these substances.

The best plan, of course, is to quit sugar (and alcohol, which health-wise is similar) by following the 7 Stability Steps in Book 6.

Supplements can help you feel better. Flaxseed oil, fish oil, and magnesium are good to take daily and may improve mood. Vitamin D3 is needed for uptake of magnesium, as well as for calcium.

Please always check with your doctor before starting to take any supplements.

Keep exercising. Working out at least three to four times a week relieves many symptoms, and is as important as all of the other suggestions combined.

Many other nutrition and supplement suggestions exist for dealing with PMS, as well as for making it through menopause without discomfort. Let's look at natural menopause strategies in the next chapter.

CHAPTER 11

DUMP SUGAR TO MINIMIZE MENOPAUSE DISCOMFORT

The brain chemical changes of menopause resemble those of PMS, including reduced serotonin and beta-endorphin. In that sense, menopause could almost be viewed as permanent PMS. (No comment.)

Perhaps the most common menopause sign is the occurrence of hot flashes. We're typically told that hot flashes can be eliminated by limiting or avoiding dairy foods, animal fats, red meat, caffeine, white flour, alcohol, and fried foods.

The most significant change you can make, however, is to eliminate sugar. That may need to include fruits. Anecdotally, I'll share that I had hot flashes only three times – always after I had indulged in fruit (beyond my usual apple per day).

Getting enough calcium is important for bone health. Nondairy sources of calcium include broccoli, kale, kelp, mustard greens, dandelion greens, turnip greens, collard greens, and sesame seeds.

The vegetables above should be eaten cooked, rather than raw. (More on that in a later chapter.)

Keep insulin secretion low to help with calcium retention. Suggestions for managing and minimizing insulin include:

- Limiting the foods in the "hot flash" list above.

- Eating only when you're hungry.

- Eating smaller meals, perhaps more frequently.

- Following the 7 Stability Steps in Chapter 29.

Phytoestrogens are another good way to alleviate menopause discomfort. Celery, parsley, nuts, and seeds contain phytoestrogens. Soy does, too, although it's a somewhat controversial food. Let's table that debate for now and include fermented soy (miso, tempeh, natto) in the phytoestrogen-containing group.

Eat ½ to 1 teaspoon of acidophilus yogurt daily. Note the small amount. Even if you're avoiding dairy, this won't be enough to cause hot flashes, and the probiotic benefits are worth it. Other probiotic foods include real sauerkraut (no vinegar, just cabbage and salt), kimchi, and even green tea.

Eat "good" fats to control cravings for sugar and other carbs. Examples are raw coconut oil, macadamia oil, walnuts, cashews, nut butters (unprocessed, no sugar), seeds, avocados, and olive oil.

Other Good Fats

Essential fatty acids are great to add to your diet. ("Essential" means we can't make it in the body and have to get it from food.) Cold-water fish, ground flaxseed or flaxseed oil, and walnuts supply a good array of EFA.

Another, somewhat surprising, source of EFA would be leafy green vegetables. We don't think of leafy vegetables as containing fats – and they don't contain much – but every bit of the fat in them is an essential fat called alpha-linolenic acid.

What About Stress and Menopause?

Chronic stress worsens symptoms, increases insulin secretion, decreases serotonin and beta-endorphin even more, induces depression, and increases appetite and food cravings. Stress management techniques can help. Stress management techniques can include, among other things, meditation, acupuncture, and heat to raise body temperature (sauna, steam, whirlpool, hot bath, or shower).

The #1 stress management technique is exercise! Here's what exercise can do:

- Raise beta-endorphin and serotonin.

- Minimize insulin secretion by making muscle more sensitive to insulin.

- Improve mood.

- Reduce insomnia, fatigue, and food cravings.

Here's to eating right and regular workouts that include some intense intervals, not just to combat menopause discomfort, but as part of a lifelong health plan.

Have you been wondering about fruit? Let's look at that next.

CHAPTER 12

HAS FRUIT ADDICTION SIMPLY REPLACED SUGAR ADDICTION?

It was, as the saying goes, déjà vu all over again.

There we were, toward the end of the day at a recent conference that featured lectures on health problems caused by gluten, health problems from free glutamate, and similar topics. The audience accepted the information enthusiastically – along with the slides that showed extremely long lists of foods that contain the offending substances. In other words, foods to avoid.

No one complained about the long lists of foods to avoid.

Finally, late in the afternoon, I gave my presentation on sugar and health. The previous speaker had run well over his limit, cutting my allotted hour down to thirty-two minutes. It would be tight but still do-able; this didn't seem like a "tough room." I began to go through my slides and my presentation points.

A man in the audience asked if I was talking about "added sugar" or was including natural products like fruit. I answered that sugar did include fruit – and that fructose, the sugar in fruit, can cause a variety of health problems.

In fact, all of the negative health consequences of sucrose – a disaccharide that's half fructose and half glucose – are attributed to the fructose in it, not the glucose.

Even though you can find disagreements in science journals on virtually everything, no disagreement on this topic exists in the science lit. Researchers all seem to agree that fructose makes sucrose the junk that it is.

Well, the man became angry and even left before the end of my short presentation. Believe me, I'd seen reactions like that before.

Since 1990, when everyone was still obsessing about fats and how bad they were said to be, sugar is a topic I've presented on many times. Audience reactions to sugar information have often been strong, and that's interesting because those were presentations, not personal consultations.

In a presentation, I have no idea what the audience members eat, so nothing can be taken personally. Or should be taken personally. But addiction isn't rational or logical.

One question in a short test for alcoholism (the CAGE) is, "Have people ever annoyed you by criticizing your drinking?" The key word in the question is "annoyed." Mess with someone's addiction, and they get angry.

Maybe we should start asking fruit addicts if people have ever annoyed them by telling them fruit is sugar.

It has seemed lately as if people don't care about sugar addiction, including their own. Fairly recently, an obese woman told me she knew she was addicted to sugar but was "okay with it."

That sounded like the 7th criterion for substance dependence in the DSM-IV. In the DSM-5, it's been split into two related criteria, but the idea remains the same: "Continued use despite adverse consequences." (The DSM-5 criteria are covered in more detail in Chapter 3.)

Everything Old Is New Again

The past fifteen years or so have shown a shift in nutrition awareness that actually harkens back to the 1970s. In the 1970s, science journals were filled with articles on the negative health impact of sugar. Films were available, and at least one popular book was written on the subject (*Sugar Blues*). In the wake of this negative publicity, the sugar industry – a powerful lobby in Washington – got busy working their evil, and, starting about 1983, several things happened:

1. Fat became the new dietary demon, and everyone started eating low-fat this and nonfat that.

2. New low- or nonfat food products were developed. Most of them included sugar to replace the fat.

3. Sugar consumption between 1984 and 1999 increased by twenty-five to forty-five pounds per person per year. Twenty-five to forty-five pounds represents the *increase*, not the total consumption. The USDA estimates current sugar consumption, which has gone up since 1999, at 156 pounds per person per year.

4. Obesity in the U.S. became an epidemic. Overweight hit a then-high of sixty-two percent.

No doubt the sugar industry was pleased with those results.

Finally, we're starting to move toward a more realistic evaluation of food:

- Fats are recognized as not being as bad as we were told – and we know some of them are supremely healthful.

- Everyone knows that sucrose is junk.

- Researchers, at least, know that fructose is what makes sucrose junk.

That last point, though, is a hard sell among the general population.

If all we've done over the past fifteen years is switch our addiction to fruit, I'm not sure we've made much progress. Especially when people get just as angry when I advise them not to eat too much fruit as they used to get when I advised them not to eat sugar.

Yet fructose is not just an addictive sugar; it also has serious health consequences. Below we'll explore the health problems associated with it.

Health Consequences of the "Healthy" Sugar

The last few chapters have dealt with aspects of sugar addiction, including sugar's effect on health.

Of course, you want to be healthy, but one topic is almost guaranteed to alienate people – talking about what's wrong with fructose. Fructose, the sugar in fruit, is nasty stuff, but we'll get to the details soon enough.

Some people are surprised that fruit could be bad. After all, it's natural. And whenever people talk about healthful eating habits, it's the first thing mentioned. "Eat lots of fruits and vegetables!" As if they're equal. Fruits even come first in that recommendation.

I agree with the recommendation in part, but suggest limiting fruit servings to one or two per day. A serving is half a cup, or a medium-size fruit. That's not much fruit, compared with vegetables. (You can go crazy with those veggies.)

The Problem With "Five a Day"

Once upon a time (pre-1991), the Basic Four Food Groups consisted of:
• Meats
• Milk Products
• Grains
• Fruits and Vegetables

The original 1991 Food Guide Pyramid was developed to give us a better idea of the relative proportions to eat. The second tier from the bottom was unevenly divided into two to four servings of fruit and three to five servings of vegetables. Apparently, that was too nuanced.

And so the slogan "Five a Day" was coined, referring to the minimum number of servings of each.

The problem lies in lumping them together. I've lost count of the clients who have used this as an excuse to get their five-a-day from fruit and skip those pesky vegetables altogether. But I digress.

Sucrose (granulated table sugar) was considered unhealthful. The fructose takeover – its use in beverages and prepared foods to replace sucrose – was actually a plot to cash in on the lower cost of fructose and the image it had as a "healthy sugar."

In reality, fructose has an extremely negative impact on health, and while some effects are relatively mild, other effects are serious.

What Does Fructose Do That's Bad for Our Health?

*   It's cariogenic, so it causes cavities.

*   It triggers sugar cravings in susceptible people.

*   It's frequently malabsorbed, leading to abdominal complaints (bloating, flatulence, diarrhea). Many people are unable to completely absorb fructose in the amounts commonly found in high-fructose corn syrup products.

Fructose can also:

*   Raise triglycerides, an independent risk factor for heart disease.

*   Cause insulin resistance in both muscle and liver, leading to diabetes.

*   Decrease glucose tolerance, leading to diabetes.

- Increase blood pressure.

- Increase LDL (bad) cholesterol – or make it smaller and denser, leading to arterial plaque formation.

- Increase blood clotting.

- Convert rapidly to body fat, particularly visceral fat, the harmful location.

- Interfere with copper absorption, which is necessary for hemoglobin.

- Be preferentially metabolized to fat in the liver and cause fatty liver disease.

- Cause hepatic (liver) inflammation.

- Damage memory and learning ability.

Whether people start with metabolic issues or not, the above changes are the expected results of increased fructose. People who respond to fructose normally show these changes at intakes of around twenty percent of total calories. Carb-sensitive people can show negative responses to as little fructose as seven percent of total calories.

Carbohydrate sensitivity is defined as exaggerated insulin secretion to sucrose. But fructose and other carbs can trigger high insulin in carb-sensitives as well.

Sucrose can cause many of these same effects. Please recall that sucrose is a disaccharide, consisting of half glucose and half fructose. All problems with sucrose are attributed to the fructose in it, not the glucose, as explained earlier. Researchers all agree that fructose is what causes the negative effects seen with sucrose.

Fructose can also increase appetite because it triggers less leptin (a key satiety hormone) and doesn't suppress ghrelin (an appetite-stimulating hormone).

Many people like to eat fruit before and after, or drink fruit juice during, exercise. But fructose is ineffective as either a pre- or a post-workout fuel. Because of the energy demands of exercise, using fructose for exercise fuel can easily lead to fructose consumption that exceeds the American daily average in a fraction of the time.

Fructose can also do even more health damage than the items listed above. For example, in diabetics, both fructose and the sweetener sorbitol (converted to fructose in the liver) accumulate in the lens of the eye, causing osmotic damage.

Even trending sugars can be junk. They include agave, maple syrup, dates, acai berries, and more. They're all fructose, and agave is highly concentrated fructose. Getting away from fructose is a wise and healthful course of action.

Because it may be difficult to do, and difficult to believe is necessary, cutting back on fructose could be seen as the final frontier in conquering sugar addiction.

Is sugar the only harmful thing we eat? How about salt? Salt still has a bad reputation – but it's one that sugar may actually deserve. Let's take a look at that.

CHAPTER 13

SALT'S OKAY? SWEET! (BUT SUGAR ISN'T....)

Chances are you know people with hypertension. It's probable that they've been told by their doctors to cut back on salt in their diets – or have been doing it on their own. After all, that's the prevailing wisdom for controlling blood pressure.

Salt contains sodium, an essential mineral that the body needs. The body uses sodium to control blood volume, for proper muscle and nerve function, and more.

Sodium is lost in sweat. The more we sweat, the more we lose. Long workouts, intense workouts or hot environments cause more sweating and sodium loss. Symptoms of low sodium can include disorientation, nausea, fatigue, even seizures or collapse.

As important as sodium levels are, it's obviously not wise to exercise while cutting back on salt intake without letting your M.D. know that you often sweat profusely while exercising. In warmer weather, this becomes even more important, even in a temperature-controlled indoor environment.

But this chapter isn't really about salt. It's about how sugar can raise blood pressure – an effect that's typically blamed on salt.

Sugar may raise blood pressure because of the increased insulin it triggers. High insulin can raise blood pressure in several ways.

- High insulin levels increase sympathetic nervous system activity, leading to vasoconstriction. That increases both heart rate and blood pressure.

- Insulin also stimulates the multiplication (proliferation) of the smooth muscle cells lining the arteries. That may narrow the size of the arterial opening (lumen) and increase blood pressure, sort of in the same way that a narrower hose can increase water pressure.

- Insulin promotes the production of serotonin, a brain chemical that's also a vasoconstrictor. Vasoconstriction can raise blood pressure, as described above. The relationship between insulin and serotonin is pretty much linear, so the more insulin secreted – say, in response to lots of sugar – the more serotonin is produced. The more serotonin, the more vasoconstriction, and so on.

- As you may recall from Chapter 8, high insulin levels can increase series 2 prostaglandins, hormones that control cellular functions. Among their numerous negative effects, Series 2 prostaglandins cause inflammation and increase blood pressure.

So What Should We Do?

- First and foremost, stay away from sugar and junky carbs. Limit alcohol. These steps will help you keep your insulin levels from skyrocketing. High insulin can and does cause hypertension, even on a low-sodium diet.

As for salt:

- Use natural, unprocessed sea salt with natural minerals, instead of refined salt.

- If your doctor has told you to modify your salt intake, don't eliminate it. We need it to replace what we lose during workouts and throughout the day. The upper limit is 2,300 mg, or 1,500 mg for older or hypertension-prone individuals. Someone who sweats profusely might be able to exceed those limits safely to a degree, but check with your doctor.

- Avoid processed foods that are loaded with sodium that we consumers can't control.

Always check with your doctor if your blood pressure is high. But keep in mind that recommendations to decrease salt may be somewhat off the mark. Sugar can – and does – increase insulin dramatically. That in turn can increase blood pressure in the ways described above. Unlike sea salt, sugar serves no important function in our diets.

We can eliminate sugar safely.

What causes cholesterol? Maybe not what you think! Find out in the next chapter how sugar can raise cholesterol.

CHAPTER 14

CHOLESTEROL: THE GOOD, THE BAD, AND THE UGLY

Cholesterol is absolutely vital for our health. It's a waxy, pearl-colored, solid alcohol that's produced primarily in the liver, but is so important that every cell in the body can make its own.

Cholesterol has several important functions:

- It's the precursor of all steroids: adrenal hormones, sex hormones, vitamin D, and bile acids.

- It helps to structure cell membranes and modifies their fluidity to compensate for diet-induced changes.

- It helps to transmit neural impulses.

- It makes skin waterproof.

- It helps to transport triglycerides.

- It can function as an antioxidant.

Calling cholesterol good or bad hinges on whether it's linked with cardiovascular disease or protects from it. Recent journal articles state that high HDL ("good") cholesterol doesn't make up for high LDL ("bad") cholesterol. Let's discuss the underlying cause of high LDL.

Many people think that eating fats raises serum cholesterol. To lower their cholesterol, they eat less fat. But dietary fat doesn't necessarily raise serum cholesterol.

What Raises Cholesterol?

Cholesterol synthesis is controlled by an enzyme (HMG-coA-reductase) that's triggered by insulin secretion. So foods that raise insulin secretion will increase serum cholesterol.

Saturated fat raises cholesterol because it stimulates insulin secretion. Unsaturated fat doesn't.

So insulin-triggering foods are more likely to increase our cholesterol than healthful fats. It's just another way that sugars and processed carbs – and the high insulin secretion they promote – turn out to be bad for us.

Good fats help us work out well and stay healthy, so knowing this is important.

It works like this. Say you've just treated yourself to a nice boiled lobster. Three ounces of lobster have 61 mg of cholesterol. As you digest, the cholesterol is released into your bloodstream. Special receptors, found in each cell, surface and pull cholesterol into the cells to be used in the various ways listed above.

As cholesterol is pulled into the cell, two things happen:

1. Cholesterol production inside the cell stops.

2. Serum cholesterol drops because the cholesterol has been transported into cells.

So eating the cholesterol in lobster won't raise your serum cholesterol.

What if you've had more than lobster? Say you've also consumed some serious insulin triggers: wine or mixed drinks, melted butter, bread and more butter, dessert.

The insulin those foods stimulate will start cholesterol production within your cells. As a result, the special receptors don't need to pull cholesterol into the cell from the bloodstream because the cell is making plenty of its own. Serum cholesterol remains high.

Why is LDL Bad and HDL Good?

HDL is a scavenger. It gathers excess LDL and takes it to the liver to be broken down, and to the intestine to be excreted.

LDL isn't really bad. It transports vital cholesterol through the bloodstream to all cells and can be pulled into those cells by the LDL receptors.

Here's the problem: Along the way, cholesterol can stick to arterial linings and create plaque formations. That negative process is atherosclerosis. The plaque itself is a combination of LDL and sticky platelets.

If you're wondering what makes the platelets sticky, sugar does a spectacular job. And the combination of higher LDL and lower HDL is written up in science journals as the expected result of a low-fat, high-carb diet.

This is important, so we don't eliminate the wrong stuff. As previously described, the many benefits of eating healthful (unsaturated) fats include enhanced endurance. Whatever your workout activity may be, cutting way back on good fats won't help you lower LDL-cholesterol. And it could hurt your endurance.

The best plan is keep the good fats, limit saturated and trans-fats, and cut down on junky carbs.

A few years ago in California, a U.S. national cycling champion taught a workshop on racing and recommended a high-sugar diet for racing season: "All the things you think you can't eat, ladies!" She listed cookies, cupcakes, pastries, donuts, and more.

While there may be special circumstances for a high-performance athlete burning 5,000 calories a day, I completely disagree with her ideas on fueling athletes. And they almost guarantee a negative effect on cholesterol, too.

I'm simply presenting a way to lower "bad" cholesterol without decreasing your endurance: Good fats can stay; bad fats and carbs should go.

And sugar is ugly.

Low-carb diets can be ugly, too. Let's see why in Chapter 15.

CHAPTER 15
WHY LOW-CARB IS BAD NEWS

Because of the bad press that carbs have received for a number of years – the new gluten-free trend is only its most recent manifestation – many people avoid carbs.

People who avoid carbs tend to define them as starches (bread, pasta, crackers, cereals, potatoes) and sugars (cakes, cookies, candy, and syrups). I include agave in the syrup group, even though few people want to acknowledge it as the sugar it is. (See Chapter 12 on fructose.)

Of course, there are plenty of other carbs out there, such as vegetables, lentils, quinoa, squash, beans, sweet potatoes and more. Many of them are good for us, particularly as fuel for training.

It's a bad idea to avoid carbs, especially if you work out regularly. Here are a few reasons for that, some of which you may already know.

Workouts

Avoiding carbs doesn't fit well with athletic training, especially tough training. In extreme cases, a low-carb diet could cause a full-fledged bonk. But even without that, low-carb eating can make it difficult, if not impossible, to reach higher heart rates in high-intensity workouts. That will limit the work you can handle, the calories you can burn, and the fitness levels you can reach.

Cardiac Issues

A very low-carb diet can lead to cardiac arrhythmia, particularly in people who train hard. If you do hard workouts, you might need to eat some starches both prior to, and following, the training. Fueling and refueling appropriately are important factors in fitness and health. In turn, the right carbs become an important factor in both.

Appetite

Eating too few starches can increase appetite. This has to do with serotonin production, which involves carbs. Serotonin gives us satiety, the feeling that we've had enough food and don't need more.

Satiety triggered by serotonin can be general, and its lack may lead to increased appetite. Satiety can also be carb-specific, so a high-carb lunch might lead to a lower-carb dinner. But someone who avoids starches as a general dietary strategy may crave lots more food in general, and/or carbs in particular.

Sugar

If you avoid starches, your cravings could lead you to sugars. (This might even be considered **Real Cravings Reason #8**.) Also, because that general feeling of satiety might not be there without the serotonin that starches help us produce, when you finally eat sugar, you might eat a lot of it. Sugar is clearly dietary trouble, and the associated health issues are outlined throughout this book.

Alcohol

Eating too few starches can lead to cravings for alcohol. The mechanism of action is the same as for sugar. Many food logs submitted by carb-phobic clients have shown low starch intake, combined with substantial alcohol consumption. Alcohol can cause a host of heath, sleep, and mood issues, as covered in a later chapter.

Insulin

If you don't increase sugar or alcohol, the long-term effects of a low-carb diet can include an up-regulation of insulin receptors. Up-regulation is sometimes misunderstood. It takes place when the level of insulin is low – say, when the diet contains few insulin-triggering foods.

In its ever-vigilant effort to maintain homeostasis, the body responds to the low level of insulin-triggering foods by increasing both the number of insulin receptors and the sensitivity of the existing ones.

That up-regulation means the body is ready to receive any insulin that's triggered and respond to it vigorously. In someone who's susceptible, that may translate to serious weight regain if and when a dieter returns to "normal" eating, even if only for a temporary period of time.

Which Carbs Are Okay?

If you need or want to avoid gluten, you can still consume healthful starches. Gluten-free starches include quinoa, lentils, beans, sweet potatoes, yams, turnips and other root vegetables, squash, and brown rice. These foods can help you avoid the problems described above and keep you exercising well, often, and as hard as you like.

More information on best diet practices is covered in Book 6. For now, let's concentrate on sugar's effects on the body.

BOOK 4

SUGAR AND YOUR BODY, PART 2

SUGAR & WEIGHT MANAGEMENT

CHAPTER 16
CALORIES IN / CALORIES OUT?
NOT ALWAYS.

A while ago, based on some long-held suspicions, I wanted to assess the accuracy of a widely held belief on weight gain and weight loss, so I ran a PubMed search. The belief is that weight management hinges on the so-called "simple arithmetic" of calories in and calories out.

Even with the limited time I had for the search, I still located nearly forty articles in various science journals that seem to challenge the calorie theory. I've categorized the results below, but need to start with a caveat. Most of the studies cited in this post were done on animals. (I've indicated specifically when the subjects were human.)

Some people will object because of that. For their benefit, I'd like to make two points:

1) Studies of this type could never use human subjects. No review board anywhere would approve research that locks people in a room,

takes all control of their food intake away from them, and forces them to gain or lose weight.

2) Are you truly prepared to state that weight management in the human body centers on calories in and calories out, while it's "anything goes" with animals? That's highly doubtful. To use just one example, knowledgeable veterinarians have confirmed that the metabolic effects of Cushing's disease, including the role of hormones in weight gain, are identical in humans and dogs.

So what happened in the studies? Dietary factors were found to disrupt the link between calorie intake and weight, and different nutrients and hormones affected the weight outcome. Here is a summary of the results:

The fat content of the diet affected weight gain and loss.

- Rats on high-fat diets developed severe obesity without over-consuming calories (four studies).

- Mice showed greater weight gained per calorie consumed (called "feeding efficiency") on high-fat versus low-fat diets (one study).

- Calorie-restricted, isocaloric (same number of calories) diets of 10% and 50% fat both reduced body weight in rats, but body fat was higher in the 50% group (one study).

- Total fat intake, rather than calorie intake, correlated with weight gain and was due principally to the saturated fat component (one study).

- Saturated fat is associated with greater weight gain than unsaturated fat (two studies).

- Fecal analysis showed that people who consume nuts regularly excrete more fat, suggesting a discrepancy in gross calorie intake and calories absorbed (one study).

The sugar content of the diet affected weight gain and loss.

• Abdominal fat deposits were caused by high-sucrose, isocaloric diets in rats, although the rats showed no differences in weight gain when compared with controls (one study).

• Rats fed sucrose plus standard chow did not eat more calories than controls on standard chow only, but gained significantly more weight per calorie consumed (feeding efficiency) and had higher body fat than controls (one study).

• Severe obesity developed in rats on a high-sugar diet and in rats on a high-fat diet, although controls eating standard chow ate significantly more calories than either the sugar group or the fat group (one study).

• In a study of human identical twins, the dietary factor isolated as causing a difference in BMI between twins was sugar intake, rather than different calorie intakes (one study).

Nutrients affected sugar-induced weight gain.

• The protein content of a high-sucrose diet was inversely related to the effects of sucrose on weight gain and feeding efficiency (one study). [Protein triggers the release of glucagon. Glucagon effects oppose those of insulin. More on insulin below.]

• Minerals added to a standard chow-plus-sucrose diet did not change the calories, but decreased weight gain and feeding efficiency and improved glucose tolerance (one study).

Insulin, a "fat storage" hormone, is a factor in weight gain.

- Rats injected with insulin gain weight with no change in diet or calorie intake (standard textbooks).

- Diet-induced insulin resistance preceded obesity development in rats (one study). [This is the opposite of what we typically read or hear.]

- In obese human subjects, insulin-resistant individuals gained less weight than non-insulin resistant individuals on diets of comparable calorie intake (three studies). This led a well-known researcher to hypothesize that insulin resistance functions as an adaptive mechanism to prevent further weight gain. A later study corroborated his hypothesis.

- A good night's sleep vs. restless sleep altered hormone balance. Restless sleep caused fat storage to increase (two studies).

- The twenty-four-hour rate of fat oxidation by skeletal muscle may be determined either by genetics or by diet. Insulin-triggering foods lower it (two studies).

- High fructose intake induces high insulin levels, which can cause weight gain (five studies).

- Chronic stress increases insulin and decreases brain dopamine, norepinephrine, and beta-endorphin. The neurochemical changes shift food preferences to carbs (specifically sugar) and lead to weight gain (nine studies).

What appears to be a balance of calories in/calories out is often the result of a change in diet composition. That, in turn, changes the hormonal response. Hormones can affect weight more profoundly than calories. (More about hormones in a later chapter.)

Despite the documentation, some of you will believe this, some will not. What I hope you'll recognize is that weight management is not just "simple arithmetic."

Note that several studies done on human subjects appear to refute thermodynamics. How would calories explain, for example, that obese, insulin-resistant individuals gain less weight than non-insulin resistant individuals on diets of comparable calorie intake?

How would calories explain that the primary dietary factor in different BMIs of human identical twins was the sugar content of their diets, rather than a difference in calorie intake?

How would calories explain that saturated fats trigger greater weight gain than unsaturated fats, when all fats provide nine calories per gram? It makes no sense from a calorie standpoint, but saturated and unsaturated fats affect hormones differently, as mentioned briefly in Chapter 14 on cholesterol. (More on this in the next chapter.)

How would calories explain weight gain associated with restless sleep versus sound sleep? Wouldn't tossing and turning all night burn more calories than sleeping soundly?

As Weight Watchers discovered, their approach of counting calories, and later points (reflecting calories), led some participants in the wrong direction – eating junk food till the calorie or point limit was reached. That contributed to the WW decision to emphasize healthful foods, rather than just a target number of calories.

It's best to shift your diet in a more healthful direction. Don't think only about calories.

Let's look at how alcohol fits in with weight management.

CHAPTER 17

ALCOHOL CAN SABOTAGE YOUR WEIGHT LOSS

It's probably unnecessary to mention that this is never a popular topic. But the impact of alcohol is significant and should be covered here, since many people consume alcohol on a regular basis.

Most people would like me to specify a range of acceptable alcohol consumption, so they know how much they can drink without consequences. If weight management is your primary concern, though, my years of experience with weight loss programs have shown that even a little can interfere with weight loss.

Alcohol can sabotage weight loss in several ways.

* *High calorie density.* Alcohol has seven calories per gram, while protein and carbs are four calories per gram. Only fats have greater density – nine calories per gram.

- *High insulin impact.* Alcohol is a short-chain molecule that triggers high levels of insulin secretion. Insulin inhibits fat oxidation, lowers the twenty-four-hour fat oxidation rate – an important factor in weight management – and promotes storage of dietary fat.

- *Effect on appetite.* Alcohol triggers the release of beta-endorphin, which inhibits the satiety center of the brain. This may result in a stronger and more frequent desire for food and a tendency to consume more at a given meal.

- *Effect on food preferences.* Alcohol's beta-endorphin release may also shift food preferences and cravings in the direction of sugars and fats. Eating more of those foods can lead to higher food and calorie intake, weight gain, and/or insulin resistance. As I've stressed in other chapters, insulin resistance isn't just the result of overweight; it can also be a cause.

- *Effect on mood.* Brain chemical changes due to alcohol may result in such negative moods as depression or anxiety, as well as insomnia and/or disturbed sleep. These can cause a variety of issues that may affect weight. Let's look at them individually.

Negative moods

Any negative mood may lead to cravings, particularly for sugars and other refined carbs, and increased food consumption.

Lower serotonin

Serotonin typically decreases with chronic alcohol use, which affects mood and increases impulsivity. That combination may make it more likely that you'll get cravings *and* have difficulty resisting them.

Sugar and calories

Eating more sugar and/or refined carbs may lead to greater calorie intake and weight gain. Perhaps worse, it can lead to further depression, other negative moods, and/or insomnia.

Disturbed sleep, lack of exercise, mood issues

Alcohol disturbs sleep by preventing the deep stages of sleep (theta- and delta-wave) that are most restorative.

Poor sleep quality can make it difficult to work out well or to show up for early morning exercise classes.

Lack of exercise can lead to depression or other negative moods in susceptible people. Lousy moods may decrease motivation to exercise altogether.

Ghrelin

Lack of sleep may also raise ghrelin levels. Ghrelin has been shown to increase appetite and food consumption while slowing metabolism.

Insulin

Because of its high impact on insulin secretion, alcohol may also result in reactive hypoglycemia, which can awaken you in the middle of the night and make it difficult to get back to sleep.

Either hypoglycemia or a lack of sleep may in turn lead to negative mood changes, cravings, and increased appetite.

As you can tell, alcohol can get in the way of even sincere attempts to lose weight. That sabotage includes, but also goes beyond, the so-called "simple arithmetic" of calories in/calories out.

What could be worse than this? Well, with the exception of calorie density, most of the factors in this chapter are true for sugar consumption, as well.

Is the desire to lose weight always realistic? Chapter 18 will cover that next.

CHAPTER 18
SIZE 6 OR SIZE 4?

Have any of your friends ever told you they want to lose weight, even though you (and everyone else) think they look perfectly fine? What advice have you given them? This chapter describes the unconventional advice I gave a nutrition client when everyone else was telling her the opposite.

The client, "Susan," came to me and complained about being a size six. She didn't like being that size and insisted that she had to be a four. Susan had been to several other nutritionists and fitness instructors, and had talked to her friends about this presumed problem. Professionals and friends alike had drawn the same conclusion. They told her she looked great the way she was (which was true; she did) and just needed to develop a more realistic view of her body.

Some people, they told her, aren't meant to be size four, and she needed to accept that.

Before making any recommendations for a client, I always ask lots of questions. That's what I did with Susan.

I took her unhappiness with her weight seriously, rather than dismissing it as a character flaw. I'm convinced that someone who feels uncomfortable at a given weight may actually be tuning in to what her body's telling her, not pining to look like her favorite fashion model.

It turned out that Susan's eating was under control for most of the day. In the evenings, she often binged.

What made the strongest impression on me was the way Susan conducted the food journal review. When she showed me her log, she went through every single entry with me. She read the foods aloud and told me the story behind everything she'd eaten at each meal. I heard about cravings, the reasons for each food selection, and more.

Obviously, Susan liked being in control. I decided that was the clue to this whole thing.

No one likes feeling out of control when it comes to food and eating. That has been the source of self-esteem issues in many clients I've worked with over the years. The main difference for Susan between sizes four and six was not her appearance, but what it *took* to be a four. To be a four, she had to control her eating. Now she was bingeing.

So we addressed what Susan ate during the day that caused her to binge at night. If you've been reading this book, it won't surprise you that the culprit seemed to be sugar. Susan's night binges always occurred after she'd eaten sugar during the day. It felt intuitively clear that getting sugar out of Susan's diet would give her back the control she really wanted, regardless of her weight.

The results showed that my hunch had been correct. Susan's cleaned-up diet didn't trigger binges, and that was a relief for her. She felt in control of herself. Yes, she did lose a few pounds. Mainly, though, she stopped obsessing about getting back to a size four.

Interestingly, Susan finally did what everyone had wanted her to do all along. She accepted her body.

If someone wants to lose weight, even if she looks pretty good, it may pay to consider her discomfort something more than an unrealistic expectation.

The next chapter deals with something I consider scary – dosing infants with sugar.

CHAPTER 19

COULD GIVING SUGAR TO YOUR BABY MAKE HER FAT?

Virtually everyone cares about babies. So I figured you'd care about babies' brains, too.

Much research has been done on rat pups and sugar. When rat pups are separated from their mothers, for example, they cry. When researchers give them sugar, they stop crying. Sugar triggers a release of beta-endorphin, which stops the distress and promotes a sense of wellbeing. Even in rat pups.

Did you know this information is being used on human infants?

Newborn infants are subjected to a variety of painful procedures – heel puncture for blood sampling and many more. The painful procedures are even more numerous and varied in pre-term newborns. Pain responses in these infants are measured by heart rate, crying time, facial activity, and other behaviors.

Sedation was once the most commonly used method for dealing with neonatal pain. That's been replaced by non-pharmacological procedures for pain relief. The procedures include pacifiers, position changes, swaddling, cradling in the arms, and reducing tactile stimulation. It's an area of disagreement and controversy.

Using sucrose has been recommended and tested, both as a stand-alone treatment and also paired with other treatments, such as pacifiers, mother's milk, and anesthetic cream.

Bottom line: Sucrose seems to be effective by itself, and all other treatments seem to work better when paired with sucrose.

I started hearing about the work on newborns and sucrose while doing research for my dissertation. I also heard it presented in a couple of seminars. It worried me then, and even more now because it's ongoing.

The problem is sugar is *not* non-narcotic.

It's only possible to consider sugar a non-narcotic intervention for newborns if you ignore its properties as an addictive drug. What are the future implications? We have an obesity epidemic now.

What might happen to obesity rates if the practice of giving sugar to babies for pain becomes so widespread that – from birth – whenever there's pain, there's sugar?

The VMH is the main satiety center in the brain, making us feel we've had enough food and don't need more. Beta-endorphin (endorphins) inhibits the satiety effect of the VMH. Inhibiting the VMH can increase food intake, especially in someone who's sensitive to the effects.

So sugar triggers beta-endorphin and inhibits the VMH. Sugar can also bring on cravings later that day, or for the next day or two. Addiction to sugar – a result of beta-endorphin and other brain chemicals – virtually guarantees that sugar intake will continue long-term, and probably increase.

If you don't take sugar seriously as an addictive drug, if you ignore its ability to increase appetite in several different ways, then this procedural stuff with infants seems harmless. And I seem like an alarmist crank. (No worries; I've been called worse.)

We would never even think of giving newborn infants narcotic painkillers. I wish we were equally cautious about sugar. It's as close to a narcotic as it can be, but easy to dismiss because it's disguised as food. (Junk food, yes, but still.)

Obviously, ending babies' pain is a good thing. Sugar seems innocent and harmless when used in that way, but it isn't.

And the obesity implications are staggering.

Chapter 20 looks at the health of pregnant women and how it affects their babies.

CHAPTER 20

SUGAR, PREGNANCY, AND AUTISM

Recently, I gave a lecture on sugar as a limiting factor in health. It was at a conference on autism and food. Autism is now referred to as autism spectrum disorder because of the widely varied symptoms that may be involved.

The disorder is absolutely *not* my field; I was speaking on sugar.

While preparing my presentation, I turned up an interesting connection. Several articles in different science journals described a link between metabolic conditions in pregnant women and their children's risk for autism spectrum disorder, developmental delays, and impaired development.

The investigated metabolic conditions included diabetes, decreased insulin sensitivity, hypertension, high triglycerides, low HDL (good) cholesterol, high fasting insulin, and high fasting glucose.

The presence of these conditions in pregnant women makes their infants more likely to develop disorders on the autism spectrum.

Metabolic Conditions and Obesity in Moms-To-Be

Researchers have concluded that rising rates of obesity among the US population could make these findings significant and quite serious in terms of public health concerns.

As described earlier, obesity can and does cause insulin resistance, but it's definitely not the only cause. A number of factors can lead to insulin resistance, including diet.

No one to my knowledge, however, is targeting the cause of these metabolic conditions at a root level – specifically, the nutrition of the pregnant women.

Diet can play a major role in the success or failure of risk management. The metabolic conditions are the same and can occur no matter which factor triggers the insulin resistance.

These metabolic conditions can be completely reversed. I've worked with obese clients and have specialized in reversing metabolic disorders through changes in nutrition and fitness for twenty years. It would be tremendously gratifying to target pregnant women, help them transform their health so they can give birth to healthy babies, and potentially reduce the incidence of autism.

There is, of course, a special twist in my approach to this issue: I can help women who are stuck in sugar addiction or other food addictions. These addictions and the cravings they cause may have stopped the moms-to-be from losing weight or reversing their metabolic conditions.

Also, as outlined in earlier chapters, sugar does more to cause high cholesterol, high blood pressure, heart disease, insulin resistance, and/or diabetes than a high-fat diet. By conquering sugar addiction, the women could be able to move forward and reverse metabolic conditions quickly.

My program, Last Resort Nutrition®, is about getting metabolic disorders under control as quickly as possible. It could make a big difference for both moms-to-be and their babies. I truly believe we can make a difference by reversing a problem that looks as if it will otherwise only get worse.

What about kids with autism? Their diets matter a lot. One striking example is described in Chapter 21.

CHAPTER 21

CAN DUMPING KIDS' SUGARY DIETS

REVERSE AUTISM?

Good results are always inspiring but sometimes go beyond words. I started working with the son of a long-standing nutrition client several years ago. The process of changing her son's nutrition took a while to do its full job, but the information she sent me a few weeks ago seemed almost miraculous.

I had worked with the mom (I'll call her Felicia) for various reasons over the years: stamina for endurance events, digestion, sleep, seasonal allergies.

Felicia's greatest concerns, though, were for her son (we'll call him Tim). He was born with a congenital heart defect that Felicia and her husband learned was one aspect of a chromosomal defect called VCFS (velo cardio facial syndrome).

As an adolescent, Tim began showing various symptoms: bipolar disorder, autism, ADHD, perseverative speech, and more. He was seen by doctors at university hospitals across the U.S., participated in NIMH studies, and was under the care of an extensive team. The team included psychiatrists, neurologists, psychologists, pediatricians, speech therapists, geneticists, and several different specialists.

The doctors prescribed an antipsychotic drug for Tim. It changed both his food preferences – he began eating junky foods with little nutrition – and his appetite. He never seemed satiated and would keep eating and eating if left on his own.

Finally, Tim was taken off the medication because it was black-labeled for patients with heart conditions. It was then that Felicia asked me to meet with him.

Felicia seemed surprised that I was able to create a rapport with Tim, and I'll admit it wasn't easy. But Tim had started playing golf and was becoming enthusiastic about athletics. I was an athlete, so that became our common ground.

My nutrition suggestions were simple and easy to follow. The great part is Tim followed them, probably to improve his sports ability. He also became my email buddy, frequently sending me questions over many months, which gave me more and more chances to help him go beyond the basic suggestions in our first few appointments.

Apparently, Tim added nutrition to the list of topics that fascinated him. Felicia told several emotional stories about his change from being "a monster in the house" to a son they could communicate with, and his call to her one afternoon to ask how her day was. He told her – for the very first time – that he loved her.

The end of this story continues to be wonderful. Tim is currently a certified personal trainer at a reputable fitness club, and his last psychiatric exam showed "no evidence of mental illness."

This astonishing transformation was made possible by increasing protein in Tim's diet, eliminating sugar and white flour, and increasing healthful fats (particularly omega-3s). Other changes along the way helped, too, but these were primary.

Tim's story is fantastic, of course. Helping him turn his life around was immensely gratifying.

And stopping autism before it even happens by helping moms-to-be improve their metabolic profiles – well, what could be better than that?

In the next chapters, we'll look at how sugar affects eating behaviors and more.

BOOK 5

SUGAR, EATING BEHAVIORS, AND MORE

CHAPTER 22

CAN JUVENILE DELINQUENTS AND BROKEN WINDOWS HELP YOU EAT LESS SUGAR? (THEY REALLY CAN!)

Giving nutrition talks in many locations lets me meet interesting people. After a recent presentation, a man came up afterward to tell me about his doctoral research.

Dull, you say? Hardly. The man was working on a program for juvenile offenders that taught them about good nutrition. His premise was that getting them to make good decisions about food would help them make better choices in life.

How Little Things Can Make a Big Difference

I was instantly reminded of Malcolm Gladwell's book *The Tipping*

Point, in which Gladwell describes the turnaround of the high crime rate in New York.

In the mid-1980s, violent crime in NYC was at a peak. Two criminologists, Wilson & Keller, theorized that crime is the inevitable result of disorder. Seemingly small displays of disorder – such as broken windows that don't get repaired – invite serious crime by signaling neglect.

The New York Transit Authority hired Keller as a consultant. Keller convinced the key players to start the crime cleanup by cleaning graffiti from the subway trains. Some thought it was a foolish start because violence on the subway trains was so high.

But the repainting of trains was relentless. Even subway cars with minimal graffiti were taken out of service until they'd been cleaned.

The message that someone was watching was clear, and it worked. The theory was then applied to other small crimes, such as fare-skipping and minor property damage. By 1990, violent crime in New York City had dropped considerably.

So What Does This Have to Do With Sugar?

What if, instead of avoiding just the big stuff – like dessert – and letting the little "tastes" slide by, we started by eliminating the little tastes? Refusing that piece of a broken cookie, those two tiny M&Ms, that agave on your oatmeal? Small tastes that seem trivial, calorie-wise.

What good would that do? Well, as you now know, sugar does affect brain chemistry and hormones, so small amounts can increase appetite and change food preferences – and not in a good way. A little can bring on cravings for sugar later that day or the next.

But What About Juvenile Offenders, Broken Windows, and Subway Trains?

I'm suggesting that strictly refusing small bits of sugar all day long could help you develop a different mindset: "That's not food."

I know from decades of counseling dieting clients that they tend to think in terms of all-or-nothing: "I ate cookies earlier, so I blew it. I'll have this chocolate cake tonight and start my diet tomorrow."

What if, instead, we get out in front of it?

Relentlessly rejecting small samplings of sugar throughout the day (and the week) could make it easier to turn down dessert.

Yes, because of the brain chemistry thing. But also this: Why undo all that careful, healthy picky-ness by blowing it on a bowl of rocky road?

Dare to Start Small: Broken Window Theory Applied to Sugar

We know sugar will continue to be around in both large and small portions.

Why not ignore the tiny tastes of sugar that will be everywhere? See if that doesn't inspire better food choices throughout the day – and throughout the year. See if it doesn't re-frame sugar as something to avoid, as the junk it is, rather than as food.

If this deceptively silly idea saves you from overdoing it on cake, pie, chocolate truffles, chocolate walnut fudge, cheesecake, and everything else that will be temptingly available as the days and weeks go on, it could even be seen as your practice.

Imagine the inner glow of having a no-sugar practice.

Besides, if you convince your friends to try this, you'll definitely be a hero, like my friend who's working with juvenile offenders. What he's doing is brilliant. And it can work for you!

What if you even got a standing ovation for throwing away sugar? Check that out in Chapter 23.

CHAPTER 23
A STANDING OVATION FOR THROWING AWAY SUGAR

Several years ago, I was on staff at a ten-day seminar on nutrition and eating behaviors. We lived at the ranch where it was held. Staff and participants alike followed the same mealtime rules.

Frankly, the seminar wasn't particularly good. But we did one great exercise that helps me to this day.

The Standing Ovation

In the dining hall, we had to stand and announce whenever we were going back to the buffet to take seconds. At that point, everyone in the room gave us a standing ovation.

The reason behind this is simple. Some people tend to pile food on their plates when they go through the buffet line. It prevents the embarrassment of returning for more. The problem is that once the food is on the plate, it's easy to keep eating, even when we don't want it.

Giving yourself permission to get seconds eliminates the need to pile extra on the plate. Start with a smaller portion, and get more only if you really need and want it.

An Even Better Standing Ovation

The other part of the exercise was this: We had to stand and announce whenever we were throwing away food. Again, everyone in the room gave us a standing ovation.

I'm convinced this is one of the most valuable exercises anyone with food issues can try.

Most of us grew up learning that it's a sin to throw away food. Didn't you? Because of the starving children, right? Where were they starving when you learned it? We all heard different countries and different locations, but the sin was the same.

Kids immediately see through this nonsense and say, "So send it to them." No one can convince kids that shoveling food into their mouths that they don't want or need will help starving children anywhere. And yet this "teaching" persists, and its negative lesson lingers into adulthood.

U.S. Food Production

Meanwhile, each and every day, the U.S. produces 3,950 calories worth of food for every man, woman, and child (even infants). This is more than most adult men need, and certainly much more than women and children need.

So, much of the food the U.S. produces is excess. There's almost no way to prevent wasting of food.

Under circumstances like these, throwing away food isn't a sin. It's survival. And learning to be 100% okay with doing it is the smartest strategy.

Convincing My Clients to Get Rid of Trouble Food

It isn't easy to convince my clients to get rid of food, especially where sugar is concerned. One client bought a giant tub of dates at Costco. Even though the sugar in the dates was triggering binges and her weight was creeping up, she kept eating them daily. When we talked about it, she said, "They're almost gone."

Perfect. Don't put the dates in the garbage. Treat your body like a garbage can and put the dates in there. Then binge. Yikes.

Another client had dinner with her parents at their home twice a week and couldn't refuse the giant portions her mother served her. She had a problem with the sin of throwing away food. I wish she'd learn to use plastic containers for the purpose for which they're intended.

Seminar Benefits You Can Use

After the seminar at the ranch – and all those standing ovations! – I can throw away any food. Now, I'm definitely *not* telling you to buy good food and throw it away for no reason.

But if a food – especially sugar – is making it difficult or impossible to stick with your eating plan, it needs to go. Not when it runs out, but now.

The impact of the sugar you can't stay away from is huge. It goes beyond the "empty calories" most people talk about when discussing sugar. (Does that phrase bore you as much as it bores me?)

Toss That Sugar

Sugar increases appetite by inhibiting your brain's satiety center. It changes your food preferences and makes you want more junk and fewer vegetables. It's addictive. It can make your eating go, and feel, out of control. As all of that happens, it affects your self-esteem, and not in a positive way.

In the U.S., sugar will – as always – be everywhere.

Stop treating your body like a garbage can. Throw junk in the real garbage can, where it belongs. If you need to ruin the food first, do it. (Dishwashing liquid is handy for that!) Dump it and move on.

Your body deserves better. So does your brain, and your self-esteem. Can you hear the standing ovation?

What do you do if you can't get food when you need it? Having a Plan B is the best strategy, as discussed in Chapter 24.

CHAPTER 24

ALWAYS HAVE A PLAN B: STABILIZE YOUR GLUCOSE (AND YOUR BRAIN) ON THE FLY!

It's dinnertime, and I'm flying home to San Francisco from a Houston business trip. The flight attendant is bringing around the service cart and I'm about to order ... milk. I never drink milk, so why now?

Let's go back to how the day started. Fortunately, I had ordered eggs and oatmeal from room service. (This was a while ago, before we all became grain-phobic.) Breakfast showed up at 7:00 a.m. So far, so good.

We were in Houston in January for a meeting called by my colleague Sherry. The meeting started at 10:00 a.m., and was scheduled to end at 1:00 p.m. My return flight was at 2:30 p.m.

Sherry had promised us food. I should have been suspicious, because Sherry and I once had dinner at an airport, and hers was a plate of white-flour pasta and a plate of white rice.

At the meeting, the only "foods" were donuts, Danish pastries, M&Ms, Halloween-size candy bars, soft drinks, and coffee. No refreshments for me, thank you.

At 1:00 p.m., a few of us got into Sherry's car so she could drive us to the airport. Six hours without food had left me hungry, and I planned to get food at the airport. Unfortunately, unexpected traffic due to an event in town slowed us to a crawl. It was not going to be possible to get food before my flight.

Maybe a pack of raw almonds? Almost every airport newsstand sells those.

Well, time was so short I had to run to the gate. As I stepped on the plane, they closed the door literally the instant I was on board.

It got worse. Due to some problem or other (believe me, I'd stopped caring), the flight couldn't take off for an hour. Even when we were cleared to go, we couldn't take off because the plane now had to be de-iced. We sat on the tarmac for two more hours.

So our 2:30 flight departed at 5:30. There was no meal service – it was an afternoon flight. A 2½-hour flight. After a 7:00 a.m. breakfast and nothing else, all I could think about was *food*.

Finally, the beverage cart appeared. I had already decided what to order. You might think I'd grab whatever I could get, but Pepsi, ginger ale, or apple juice would have spelled nothing but trouble for a carb-sensitive like me.

The answer lay in finding food.

Food on a beverage cart. Are you thinking peanuts? So was I, but they had pretzels. White flour would have been worse than nothing. My plan (at this point, I think I had gone beyond Plan B to Plan C or D) was milk. Milk isn't a beverage; it's food. Usually, I don't drink it, but this wasn't usual.

Got milk? They had it – two percent, the only kind they serve on airlines. I had done the calculations – having had plenty of time for arithmetic while sitting on the tarmac – and two percent milk was the only reasonable solution. It came as close to a 40-30-30 meal as I could get on the fly, although it was light on protein and a bit heavy on fat. Even though I don't go around pushing 40-30-30 meals (remember *The Zone*?) on my clients, I do know that those percentages are stabilizing.

The key word is "stabilizing," and that's the take-away here. In this case, stability refers to both glucose (blood sugar) and brain chemicals. In a semi-emergency like this, it's tempting to use the situation as an excuse to grab anything edible, even junk.

But milk was a wiser choice, and in twenty minutes I felt a lot better.

Lately, I've been finding it necessary to go with Plan B often – so the best idea is always to have one. When it comes to food, a solid Plan B is absolutely vital.

Carry envelopes of protein powder or packs of raw nuts with you, rather than fruit or granola bars. Think stability. After all, we're talking about your brain first, as well as the rest of you.

Speaking of your brain, do you know people who are on raw diets? Raw food diets may be wrong for you, as you'll find out in the next chapter.

CHAPTER 25
WHY SUGAR ADDICTION AND RAW FOOD
DIETS MAY NOT MIX

I'm often asked for my opinion about raw food diets, so I've done a great deal of thinking about them. Here's what I think.

On the surface, it seems reasonable that raw foods would be better for us. After all, every process we put our food through, from start to finish, detracts a little (sometimes a lot) from the nutrition. Raw foods would undergo the least processing, so it seems they'd be more nutritious. Perhaps because of that, many raw foodies say they feel more energetic on a raw diet.

A couple of problems may occur with raw diets, though.

Goitrogens

One has to do with substances called goitrogens that some foods contain. Goitrogens can interfere with thyroid function, making it wise to limit or even avoid foods that contain them.

Which foods contain goitrogens? The list includes cabbage, pine nuts, broccoli, Brussels sprouts, kale, spinach, bok choy, cauliflower, mustard greens, collards, radishes, turnips, peanuts, soy, and more.

As you know, some of these foods have a well-deserved reputation for being nutrition-packed all-stars, so we don't necessarily want to eliminate them.

The good news is that heat from cooking can effectively destroy goitrogens, so the healthful foods in the list above can still be part of your diet if you release them from the raw rule. I was in the habit of juicing several of these foods, and when I learned about goitrogens, I stopped. Now I always steam or saute those foods. In the case of soy, fermentation (miso, tempeh) will do the trick.

Vegetables or Fruits?

Another problem I've seen has to do with which "track" the raw foodie chooses. It actually appears to be quite clear-cut: Some raw foodies go in the vegetable direction, some in the fruit direction. It's the fruit direction that concerns me.

Health-wise, fructose, the sugar in fruit, is nasty stuff. Health consequences of fructose are outlined in Chapter 12.

Fructose doesn't stimulate leptin (an important satiety hormone). It doesn't suppress ghrelin (a powerful, appetite-stimulating hormone). Those two facts mean fructose may increase appetite. It's addictive, can promote sugar cravings, and can cause malabsorption and gastro-intestinal disturbances.

Fructose is also a relatively ineffective training fuel, either pre- or post-training.

- It absorbs less rapidly than glucose during exercise.
- It promotes less water uptake, leading to dehydration.
- It blocks sodium absorption.
- It replaces glycogen poorly.

Raw foodies who favor fruit tell me how great it is to "eat raw" because they "can have pie for breakfast," and it's perfectly healthful because it's raw. The pie shell is typically made from crumbled nuts, while the pie filling is fruit puree. Variations on this theme can be found in stores. Whole Foods, for example, sells cookies that resemble Oreos, with a cookie made of crumbled nuts and filled with a paste-like fruit puree. Stop!

The Smarter Way to Do Raw

The advantages of raw food diets would seem to lie in the consumption of lots of vegetables, along with the elimination of unwholesome foods. Someone who goes from eating lots of cakes, desserts, bread, and other sugar- or gluten-containing foods to eating plenty of raw vegetables will undoubtedly experience a noticeable shift in health, weight, energy, and symptom management.

If you've already made beneficial changes in your diet and don't eat much junk of any kind, you'll probably notice a less dramatic change when switching to raw foods. Even a subtle change may feel worth it to you, however, so make your own decision.

If you decide to switch to a raw diet, please do yourself a big health favor and follow these simple suggestions:

- Cook foods that contain goitrogens.

- Get on the raw vegetable track, rather than the fruit track.

- Don't skimp on protein. Raw vegetable protein powder is available and critical for your success.

Fructose is sugar, no mistake about it. In quantity, fruit and fructose can pack quite a mean punch. The fact that they're raw won't change that. Please don't look for a loophole.

Speaking of loopholes, do you know that product developers use them on food labels to fool us? More information on that is in Chapter 26.

CHAPTER 26

LABELING LOOPHOLES HELP SUGAR SNEAK INTO YOUR FOOD

Labeling loopholes are ways that product developers get away with less-than-full disclosure on the labels of our foods. Let's look at just two labeling loopholes.

Loophole #1: Glycerin / Glycerol

Glycerin (or glycerol) is a "polyol," a form of alcohol. It's not like ethanol, so it won't give you a buzz, but it is an alcohol.

Glycerin is used as a sweetener. Maybe you haven't heard of it or paid much attention to it, but it's in many foods – including about 99.999% of those convenient food bars that are far too numerous to name individually. Glycerin will always be shown in the ingredient lists because the FDA insists, but that's where the disclosure seems to end.

Things may get fuzzy once you check the nutrient counts. If you were ever geeky enough (yes, that would describe me) to do the arithmetic and calculate the calories of fat, carbs, and protein in a glycerin-containing food bar, you might notice a discrepancy between the carb numbers you calculated and the label count of carbs per serving.

According to Mendosa.com's Diabetes Update, about half the glycerin-containing bars that were tested had inaccurate nutrient counts.

Why is that? Glycerin doesn't fall into the reported categories. Strictly speaking, it's not a carb, not a protein, not a fat, so it doesn't have to be counted in with any one of them.

That technicality allows the product developers and packagers to make claims on the label. They can say "low carb" or "no carbs." They can say "low sugar" or "sugar-free." The claims are considered true because glycerin isn't any of those.

But it's definitely a sweetener – and often high on the list of predominant ingredients. The product developers know that, of course, but are willing to keep consumers in the dark because it might limit sales if everyone understood how much sweetener the bars contain. Don't be fooled.

Loophole #2: Sneaky Listing of Ingredients

A second labeling trick is how sugars are placed on ingredient lists. Several food bars use a variety of sugars and other sweeteners, but each of them is listed on the label as a separate ingredient.

I'll blow the whistle on Cliff Bars because I've counted between nine and thirteen different sugars on their labels. At my last count, this applied to every Cliff Bar, no exceptions.

This labeling practice may encourage "casual" label readers to skip over the sugars they don't recognize (such as cane juice), or simply keep them unaware of how much total sugar is in the bar.

If all the sugar in the bar came from the same source, it would have to appear first on the list as the predominant ingredient. Separating the sugars prevents that.

Product developers are paid to know these things and help food companies take advantage of it (and us). Remaining aware is the only way to prevent it.

In Book 6, we'll look first at how to stop a sugar craving in its tracks – and then move on to defeating sugar addiction permanently.

BOOK 6

RECOVERY RX

• *SHORT-TERM CRAVINGS ELIMINATION*

• *LONG-TERM PLAN FOR CONQUERING SUGAR ADDICTION*

CHAPTER 27

THE CRAVINGS ELIMINATION PLAN

In the same way that weight-loss plans are everywhere these days, so are plans for eliminating sugar cravings.

Many of them stress that sugar cravings will simply go away if you turn your attention to something else, or change the scenery by talking a walk.

Some suggest that you meditate. Some say drink water. Some tell you to avoid stress. Some recommend talking to a friend.

Some plans suggest eating a little of the craved food, and then turning your attention to something else.

One variation suggests eating the sugar you crave plus something healthful.

Some suggest eating fruit.

Some suggest eating an extremely decadent and delectable version of the food you crave and savoring it.

I don't endorse any of those. No surprise.

You don't want to *mask* the cravings. You don't want to *postpone* them. You want to *eliminate* them.

In this book, I've suggested that sugar cravings have a lot to do with brain chemistry, so changing brain chemistry is the primary way – maybe the best way – to get rid of the cravings.

Eating some sugar – even fruit – is likely to result in a priming-type effect and the desire for more. If you eat sugar, the craving will go away for a while but then come back with a vengeance.

So sugar, or substitutes like fruit, may be a bad idea.

Nutrition Magic to Trample Those Cravings

You have a sugar craving *now*, and you want to get rid of it *now*.

How do you do it? This is a job for Super B!

B vitamins are the key players in the only *nutrition magic* I know. If you have a craving – for sugar, white flour, alcohol, nicotine, or almost anything – a teaspoon of **liquid B-complex** can take it away within minutes.

Please read the above advice correctly. I'm suggesting a complete B-complex liquid supplement. It does *not* say B12!

For some reason that defies understanding, people hear me say "complete B-complex" and interpret that as "B12."

B12 is only part of the complete B-complex – and not even the most important of the B vitamins when it comes to ending cravings. But this misinterpretation happens so often it seems necessary to mention it specifically.

So, if you choose to try this, please get a complete B-complex supplement. Get liquid because it works quickly.

It definitely takes self-discipline to reach for a teaspoon of liquid B-complex when you crave sugar, but it's quite effective and can truly feel like magic.

Liquid B-complex can end the craving within a few minutes. That doesn't seem possible, but it's true. As I said, it feels like magic. And it's truly the only nutrition magic I know.

If you can, try to find a B-complex without fructose in it. I have a brand that I use and recommend, but my concerns are the liability issues that might stem from recommending a specific product in a book.

In any case, before you try liquid B-complex, check with your doctor and find out if B vitamins are safe for you. In high doses, some B vitamins can cause side effects, ranging from diarrhea to liver dysfunction, with a lot in between. Also, some B vitamins may interact with certain medications.

For these reasons, I recommend B-complex as a short-term solution *only*. No matter what, the safest thing is always to *check with your doctor* before you try this or any other supplements.

CHAPTER 28

STRONGER THAN SUGAR: TRIUMPH OVER SUGAR ADDICTION

The long-term plan must involve changing your diet, and I'm fully aware that it can be easier said than done. But it really is the only way.

If you're serious about triumphing over sugar addiction, trouncing those sugar cravings permanently, and transforming your health, your moods, your weight, and how you feel about yourself, please remember that eating sugar can and will make you want more.

The less sugar you eat, the better you'll do when it comes to conquering – permanently! – the cravings that may have held you back in the past.

Before we go through the full plan, though, I need to caution you.

"Tapering" Sugar Is Not the Solution (No Matter Who Says It Is!)

In the years (okay, decades) that I've been helping people conquer sugar addiction, some clients have balked at the idea of giving up sugar all at once: cold turkey, as it's known. They wanted to wean themselves off sugar a bit at a time.

Experience has taught me that the tapering approach doesn't work for a number of reasons. Yes, some sugar-users get results by tapering, but just about everything works for *some* people. Serious addicts may never get themselves off sugar completely if they feel they can get away with a little bit. That little bit can cause problems.

Relapse

It's easy for sugar addicts to rebound and relapse when they still have sugars – even sneaky ones – in their diets. This can be attributed to the priming-type effect I've already described, where a little makes us want more. Some "experts" claim that priming doesn't happen with sugar (the term came from drug addiction literature), but decades of clinical experience have shown me it absolutely does.

Clients have told me that starting the day with orange juice, for example, sets them up to crave sweet foods all day long. Frankly, I don't care if the clients can cite a reference in a science journal; I just listen to them and help them conquer their sugar addiction.

Loophole Thinking (Not the Label Kind)

As a result of continuing to eat sugar in small amounts, addicts may start looking for loopholes – substitutes for sugary foods or ways to sneak sugar into their diets. They begin eating extra dairy or using agave or artificial sweeteners while telling themselves they're "off" sugar.

Some substitutes can be addictive in themselves. I had a client who was even more hooked on aspartame than she was on "real" sugar. Other sugar addicts use diet colas for their fix. And we've already blown the whistle on fruit sugar, fructose. It could be the worst of all – and makes sucrose the junk we know it is.

Tastes Won't Change

Sugar addicts who taper may never acquire a taste for healthful foods. Their tastes are still oriented toward sweet, although maybe in smaller amounts than they used to eat.

This is especially true where vegetables are concerned. I'm forever encouraging my clients to eat lots of vegetables (just ask them), but the ones who are most severely addicted to sugar typically say they hate vegetables. The reason is obvious: vegetables aren't sweet.

Again, this is why I'm against that five-a-day rule. It's supposed to refer to fruits and vegetables, but sugar addicts will turn that into all fruits, given the chance.

Excess Insulin

Advocates of tapering don't seem to know that sugar addiction is often grounded in carbohydrate sensitivity. Carb-sensitive people release lots of insulin when they eat sugar, including sugar found in fruit and syrups. Artificial sweeteners can trigger insulin and endorphins (beta-endorphin) in carb-sensitive folks, as well.

Carb sensitivity is not the only factor in sugar addiction, but it can be directly related to health issues. For optimal health, we want to release just enough insulin to do the job and no more. Excess insulin has been associated with a large number of diseases – most of the ones we tend to die from in the US.

The Bottom Line

To sum up, I don't endorse a tapering plan that encourages semi-recovery from sugar addiction, even temporarily, because it can result in:

- Priming.
- A diet that's still oriented toward sweet foods.
- Long-term preference for fruits (and other sugars) over vegetables.
- Continued cravings.
- Excess insulin if the substitute foods are big insulin triggers.
- Possible relapse.

I want better for you. I want you to gain optimal health *and* the self-confidence that comes from knowing you didn't just stop using sugar halfway (and maybe relapse), but conquered it completely.

Your Long-Term Plan to Make You Stronger Than Sugar

The key to long-term triumph over sugar addiction is *stability* – stabilizing your glucose (blood sugar) and your brain chemistry.

Protein and good fats are your stabilizing foods.

When you begin asking, "Will this stabilize me or de-stabilize me?" before you eat any food, you'll definitely be on the right track!

The 7-Step Stability Plan in the next chapter was designed to be easy to follow. Don't let its simplicity fool you. It's based on years of research and clinical experience, and was created for you.

CHAPTER 29
YOUR 7 STABILITY STEPS

1. **Move more! Exercise four or more days per week.**

   This provides a good brain chemistry shift *and* a metabolic boost that makes your muscles more sensitive to insulin. Don't skip this; it's key. Be sure your workout includes some high-intensity intervals.

2. **Eat at regular intervals – no longer than four to five hours without food.**

   Don't skip eating. Always take food with you, just in case.

3. **Eat protein with everything**, except once a day (see Step 6 below).

   Protein foods include: fish, chicken, beef, turkey, shrimp, crab; yogurt with 18-20 g of protein per serving; vegetable protein powder (unsweetened).

   Carry an envelope of protein powder or other protein with you, just in case.

4. **Eat fat with everything**, except once a day (see Step 6 below).

Eat good fats in moderate portions. Don't fear them; don't overdo them.

Good fats include: fish oil, walnuts, raw coconut oil, ground flax seed, avocado, olive oil, raw nuts, macadamia nut oil.

5. **Eat the best carbs.**

"Best carbs" are mostly vegetables (6 to 13 servings of ½ cup each).

Eat complex starches for the rest (quinoa, sweet potato, lentils, brown rice, turnips, pumpkin & other squash, beans).

Limit fruit to one or two servings of ½ cup a day.

Avoid sugar and white flour.

Avoid alcohol.

6. **Eat one all-starch snack per day.**

This is another good brain chemistry shift (toward serotonin) to help you fall asleep easily and sleep soundly. Serotonin has a relaxing effect and is the precursor of melatonin, the sleep hormone and an anti-inflammatory.

Have this snack about 60-90 minutes before bed for best sleep.

Select complex starches (see Step 5 above).

7. **Drink at least eight to ten glasses of water** per day, every day.

Drink even more if you've exercised. Urine should be pale in color.

A Simple Way to Use the 7 Stability Steps

→ Construct your meals and snacks with one food from each group:

- Protein
- Vegetables (6-13 servings) <u>or</u> fruit (1-2 servings)
- Complex starch
- Unsaturated fat

→ Don't treat your snacks as if they're different from meals. Just think of them as small meals and "build" them the same way.

→ The Stability Plate diagram below shows how to construct a good meal or snack.

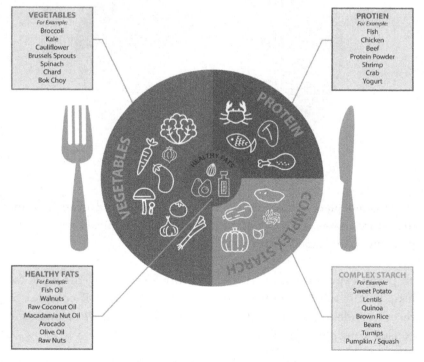

→ If you're not ready to handle vegetables at breakfast, it's okay to substitute fruit for veggies. I have vegetables with breakfast all the time now, but you might need to ease into that.

But!!

→ *Do not* cover half your plate with fruit. Limit the fruit to one serving – that's ½ cup or one medium-size fruit – and put the rest of the meal together as shown.

NOT READY FOR VEGGIES AT BREAKFAST JUST YET?

→ Divided plates with lids are available online and even in some drugstore chains. They can make it easy to prepare meals and to carry your meals and snacks with you to work.

→ If you experience *any* cravings for *any* food during the week (or less) that it takes to quit sugar, just take the liquid B-complex as recommended in Chapter 26 for short-term cravings. (Remember to consult your physician first.)

Stay strong – the results will be more than worth it!

CHAPTER 30
WHAT'S NEXT?

Stopping your consumption of sugar completely and permanently is something that may take ongoing support and further education beyond the help that a short book can provide.

Here are some suggestions for your continued success:

Your Next 7 Success Steps

1. Keep doing what got you results in the first place.

It's easy to think the problem is solved, or over, but addicts know they have to stay with the process over the long haul. Sugar addiction is no different. The most important thing is to stay with it.

2. Prepare yourself for success.

Keep a bottle of liquid B-complex on hand for those days that you do get a craving. You might even want to keep one bottle at home and one at work.

3. Stay aware.

Read labels all the time. Know what's in every food you buy – or are about to buy. Don't bring the junk home and then try to resist it. Just don't.

4. Refuse to lose the battle.

Don't let friends or family sabotage you. The words "A little bit can't hurt you" are dangerous words for a sugar addict. Tiny tastes and sneaky sugars can, and do, affect us.

5. Get expert assistance and education.

To help you conquer sugar long-term and finally achieve the freedom you've longed for and the health you deserve, I offer a program called Last Resort Nutrition®.

Last Resort Nutrition® is a proven program that has worked for thousands of people just like you. It can take you from where you are now to where you want to be with food and your health.

Last Resort Nutrition® gives you time-tested strategies and tactics that you can follow step by step – tools for controlling your appetite, cutting cravings, and changing food preferences easily, without struggle.

6. Get an expert coach.

Anthony Robbins said, "Knowledge is only potential power. Implementation is power." Nutrition coaching from someone who understands sugar addiction is implementation on steroids!

You know I get it. You know I won't tell you it's your imagination, or that you should just think about something else.

You'll get a detailed execution plan so you can *take action and get results* as quickly and easily as possible.

7. Keep exercising!

Exercise guidelines are beyond the scope of this book, but working out regularly – 3 or more times per week – is absolutely essential for your continued success. Even a short workout can work wonders, especially if it includes some high-intensity intervals of 20 to 40 seconds.

As an exercise physiologist with 30 years in the fitness industry, I can coach you by offering effective workout guidelines so you can transform your health and your weight.

Why stay "locked" in health issues when you can get moving in the right direction now? I'm committed to helping you do that!

Imagine...

- Being free of sugar addiction.
- Eating right without struggling to do it.
- Returning from your doctor's office with a great report.
- Losing weight and improving your health.
- Increasing your chances of a long and healthy life with your family.
- Having the energy to do what you want to do.
- Being fit and active and not worrying about your health.
- Feeling empowered and self-confident because *you* made it all happen.

Ending sugar addiction can help you improve your moods, transform your health, and lose weight, even if diets haven't worked for you. Once you're unstuck, you'll be able to improve your health and even potentially stop medications (always with your doctor's approval).

To start your next success steps, please visit my websites:

www.lastresortnutrition.com

www.foodaddictionsolutions.com (under Services>Coaching).

Made in the USA
Middletown, DE
11 July 2020